RECOURCES

Dilators

Amielle Comfort

For use with vaginismus, vulvodynia, postnatal sexual pain or after pelvic surgery.

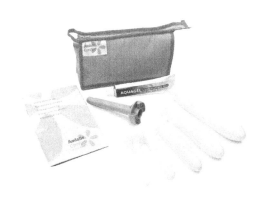

Amielle Care

(for use after radiation)

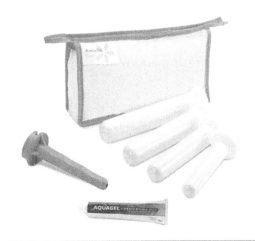

For more informations visit:

www.owenmumford.com

Lubricants

For vaginal training I recommend pjur® med lubricants. These products are all ideal for hyper-sensitive, dry and stressed skin and guarantee long lasting lubrication.

For more informations visit our homepage

moyosecrets.info or visit www.pjurmed.com

Note:
These products are only recommandations. Feel free to purchase and use your own favorite products.

For more information please visit:

MOYOSECRETS.INFO

REFERENCES

Yitzchak M. Binik. The DSM Diagnostic Criteria for Dyspareunia; Springer 2009. The DSM Diagnostic Criteria for Vaginismus; Springer 2009

Dyspareunia Looks Sexy on First But How Much Pain Will It Take for It to Score? A Reply to My Critics Concerning the DSM Classification of Dyspareunia as a Sexual Dysfunction. Archives of Sexual Behavior, Volume 34, Number 1, February 2005, 63–67

Should Dyspareunia Be Retained as a Sexual Dysfunction in DSM-V? A Painful Classification Decision. Archives of Sexual Behavior, Volume 34, Number 1, February 2005, 11–21

Kimberley A. Payne, Sophie Bergeron, Samir Khalifé, Yitzchak M. Binik. Assessment, Treatment Strategies, and Outcome Results: Perspective of Pain Specialist. 12-Goldstein-chs12-ppp, August 2005, 473–481

Physical Therapy for Vulvar Vestibulitis Syndrome: A Retrospective Study. Journal of Sex & Marital Therapy, 2002, 28: 183–192

Alessandra Graziottin. Sexual Pain Disorders: Dyspareunia and Vaginismus in: Porst H. Buvat J. (Eds), ISSM (International Society of Sexual Medicine)Standard Committee Book, Standard Practice in Sexual Medicine, Blackwell, Oxford, UK, 2006, 342–350

Gayle Watts, and Daniel Nettle. The Role of Anxiety in Vaginismus: A Case-Control Study Newcastle University, Institute of Neuroscience, Newcastle, United Kingdom, June 2009, 1–6

Tessa Crowley, David Goldmeier, Janice Hiller. Diagnosing and Managing Vaginismus- British Medical Journal, June 2009

M. Mousavi Nasab, Z. Farnoosh- Management of Vaginismus with Cognitive – Behavioral Therapy, Self-Finger Approach: A Study of 70 Cases- Iranian Journal of Medical Sciences, Volume 28, June 2003, Number 2, 69–71

T. Y. Rosenbaum- The Role of Physiotherapy in Sexual Health: Is it Evidence-Based? Urogynecological Physiotherapy, Tel Aviv and Jerusalem, Israel, Journal of the Association of Chartered Physiotherapists in Women's Health, Autumn 2006, 1–5

Musculoskeletal Pain and Sexual Function in Women. Inner Stability, Urogynecological Physiotherapy, Bet Shemesh, Israel, 2009, 1–6

Pelvic Floor Involvement in Male and Female Sexual Dysfunctionand the Role of

Physiotherapy Private Practice, Tel Aviv and Jerusalem, Israel, Journal of Sex Medicine, 2007, 4: 4–13

Rosenbaum T. Y., and Owens. AThe Role of Pelvic Floor Physical Therapy in the Treatment of Pelvic and Genital Pain-Related Sexual Dysfunction. Journal of Sex Medicine, 2008, 5: 513–523

Kimberly A. Fisher. Management of Dyspareunia and Associated Levator Ani Muscle Overactivity; Physical Therapy, 2007, 87: 935–941

E. Lambreva, R. Klaghofer, C. Buddeberg. Psychosoziale Aspekte bei Patientinnen und Patienten mit sexuellen FunktionsstörungenPraxis, 2006, 95: 226–231

Made in the USA
Coppell, TX
30 October 2019

TEXAS TEST PREP
Practice Test Book
STAAR Reading
Grade 5

ISBN 978-1500629328

CONTENTS

Section 1: Reading Mini-Tests

INTRODUCTION TO THE READING MINI-TESTS
For Parents, Teachers, and Tutors

How Reading is Assessed by the State of Texas

The STAAR Reading test assesses reading skills by having students read passages and answer questions about the passages. On the STAAR Reading test, students read 4 or 5 literary or informational passages, as well as 1 or 2 sets of paired passages. Students answer a total of 44 multiple-choice questions.

About the Reading Mini-Tests

This section of the practice test book contains passages and question sets similar to those on the STAAR Reading tests. However, students can take mini-tests instead of taking a complete practice test. Each mini-test has either one literary passage, one informational passage, or a set of paired passages. Students answer 10 to 12 multiple-choice questions about the passage or passages.

This section of the book is an effective way for students to build up to taking the full-length test. Students can focus on one passage or pair of passages and a small set of questions at a time. This will build confidence and help students become familiar with answering test questions. Students will gradually develop the skills they need to complete the full-length practice tests in Section 3 and Section 4 of this book.

Reading Skills

The STAAR Reading test assesses a specific set of skills. These skills are described in the TEKS, or Texas Essential Knowledge and Skills. The full answer key at the end of the book identifies the specific skill that each question is testing.

STAAR READING

Mini-Test 1

Informational Text

Instructions

This set has one passage for you to read. Read the passage and answer the questions that follow it.

Choose the best answer to each question. Then fill in the circle for the best answer.

Playing a Musical Instrument

Playing a musical instrument is a popular pastime for all age ranges. Young or old, it is lots of fun to play a musical instrument. There are many different types to choose from including guitar, flute, piano, trumpet, and saxophone.

Making a Choice

First, you need to choose a musical instrument that you would like to learn how to play. Here are some things you should think about:

- the cost of the instrument
- how easy or difficult the instrument is to learn
- whether there is a teacher available to help you learn it
- what opportunities there will be to play it

You might also think about the kind of music you'd like to play. This will probably be the kind of music that you also enjoy listening to.

Another thing to consider is whether you'd like to play music alone or as part of a group. If you want to play alone, you might like to play the piano. This would not be a great choice if you'd like to play in a marching band! A trumpet or a trombone would be a better choice for that. If you'd like to play in a small group, you might choose the violin or the cello. String instruments like these are often played together in groups of two to four musicians. If you're imagining playing in a rock band, the guitar or the drums are popular choices. If you imagine yourself playing in a huge orchestra, you have lots of choices. You could play anything from the flute, to the saxophone, to the piano or the drums.

One other thing to consider is whether you would also like to sing as well. Some instruments are great for this, while others are not so good. It would be nearly impossible to sing while playing the trumpet! If you want to sing as well, consider learning the piano or the guitar. Just remember that you will have to work hard on your singing skills as well as your playing skills.

Getting Your Gear

Now you have chosen your instrument, you need to buy it. If it is expensive, you might like to borrow it instead. You might know a friend or relative who plays an instrument. You can ask to borrow an instrument for a little while to try it out. That way, you can make sure it is the right choice before spending lots of money. Some schools or libraries will lend students instruments. Or you can look in your local paper or online for a secondhand instrument.

Getting Ready to Learn

After you have your instrument, you should then create a learning plan. This might involve private lessons with a music teacher or going to music classes. Some people choose to learn on their own. You can use books, movies, web sites, or you can even watch videos online.

To learn quickly, your plan may include a variety of learning methods. Make sure that you attend every lesson or study your books regularly. Also, be sure to practice what you have learned as this is the best way to develop your new skill.

Making Music

Once you have learned enough to play a song, you should start playing for people. Many people get nervous when they first start performing. You might find that you make more mistakes than usual. Don't let this get you down. Remember that you will learn to calm and control your nerves the more you practice. It is often a good idea to start with your family or friends. Or you might play for your music class. Once you become confident, you can then play for larger groups of people.

Keep Going

To become a good musician, you have to keep playing. Keep learning as much as you can and practice often. Challenge yourself to learn more difficult songs as well. As you learn more, you will become better and better. Some people even become good enough to play music as a career.

1   Read this sentence from the passage.

Playing a musical instrument is a popular pastime for all age ranges.

What does the word <u>pastime</u> mean?

Ⓐ   Choice

Ⓑ   Career

Ⓒ   Sport

Ⓓ   Hobby

2   According to the passage, what should you do first?

Ⓐ   Check to see if your school will lend you an instrument

Ⓑ   Decide what instrument you would like to play

Ⓒ   Create a plan for learning to play an instrument

Ⓓ   Look in your local newspaper for an instrument

3   Under which heading is information provided about deciding what type of instrument to learn to play?

Ⓐ   Making a Choice

Ⓑ   Getting Your Gear

Ⓒ   Getting Ready to Learn

Ⓓ   Making Music

4 Which instrument mentioned in the passage has a name based on a Greek root meaning "sound or voice"?

Ⓐ Saxophone

Ⓑ Trumpet

Ⓒ Trombone

Ⓓ Violin

5 The web below lists ways that people can learn to play a musical instrument on their own.

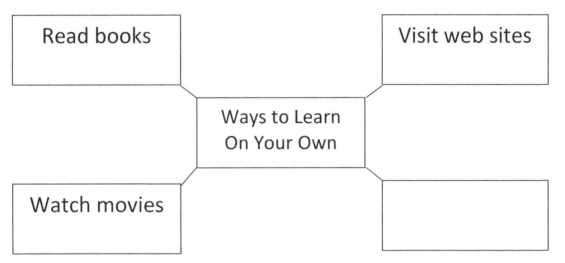

Which of these best completes the web?

Ⓐ Watch videos online

Ⓑ Attend a class

Ⓒ Find a tutor

Ⓓ Go to concerts

6   What is the main purpose of the passage overall?

ⓐ   To compare different musical instruments

ⓑ   To persuade people to join a musical group

ⓒ   To teach people how to play a musical instrument

ⓓ   To give people advice about learning to play music

7   Read this sentence from the section "Making Music."

It is a good idea to start with your family or friends.

Why does the author most likely suggest starting with your family or friends?

ⓐ   So your friends will want to learn to play as well

ⓑ   So your family will see that you are trying hard

ⓒ   So you feel more comfortable playing

ⓓ   So you can have people join in

8   Which sentence from "Making Music" tells how to solve the main problem described in the section?

ⓐ   *Once you have learned enough to play a song, you should start playing for people.*

ⓑ   *Many people get nervous when they first start performing.*

ⓒ   *You might find that you make more mistakes than usual.*

ⓓ   *Remember that you will learn to calm and control your nerves the more you practice.*

9   Why does the author use bullet points in the passage?

Ⓐ   To highlight the main points

Ⓑ   To list a set of ideas

Ⓒ   To show steps to follow in order

Ⓓ   To describe items that are needed

10   The photograph of the girl at the end of the passage is probably included to suggest which of the following?

Ⓐ   How much time and effort it takes to become good at playing

Ⓑ   How it is best to choose an instrument you can play on your own

Ⓒ   How enjoyable and rewarding playing an instrument is

Ⓓ   How it can be difficult to play for an audience at first

STAAR READING

Mini-Test 2

Literary Text

Instructions

This set has one passage for you to read. Read the passage and answer the questions that follow it.

Choose the best answer to each question. Then fill in the circle for the best answer.

Spinning the Spider's Web

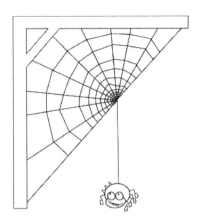
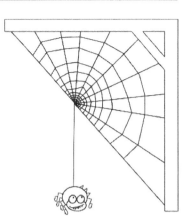

The spider spins his silken web,
In the corner of my home,
He weaves it for his family,
One teeny space their own.

I watch him as he toils,
Through the hours of the day,
Spinning as the summer burns,
Forever building come what may.

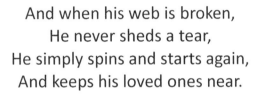

And when his web is broken,
He never sheds a tear,
He simply spins and starts again,
And keeps his loved ones near.

This small kingdom is his castle,
And a tiny place to rest,
Although some may beg to differ,
He builds his home to be the best.

He goes about his business,
And does not seek to pry or scare,
He means no harm to those around him,
To cross your path, he wouldn't dare.

The spider just keeps on spinning,
His winding, silken web,
Building homes amongst the darkness,
Keeping family in good stead.

So next time you see the spider,
Spinning webs inside your home,
Think how hard he has to toil,
Without a single word or moan.

1 Read this line from the poem.

I watch him as he toils,

What does the word <u>toils</u> mean?

Ⓐ   Works

Ⓑ   Spins

Ⓒ   Struggles

Ⓓ   Plays

2 In the poem, the speaker both observes the spider and infers the spider's thoughts and feelings. Which pair of lines is an example of the speaker inferring the spider's thoughts and feelings?

Ⓐ   *The spider spins his silken web,*
             In the corner of my home,

Ⓑ   *I watch him as he toils,*
             Through the hours of the day,

Ⓒ   *He goes about his business,*
             And does not seek to pry or scare,

Ⓓ   *The spider just keeps on spinning,*
             His winding, silken web,

3 What does the poet seem to find most impressive about spiders?

Ⓐ   That they can live anywhere

Ⓑ   That they never stop working

Ⓒ   That they are not afraid of anything

Ⓓ   That they leave people alone

4   Which stanza of the poem has a message about facing disappointments?

Ⓐ   Stanza 1

Ⓑ   Stanza 2

Ⓒ   Stanza 3

Ⓓ   Stanza 4

5   Which literary technique does the poet use in the first line of the poem?

Ⓐ   Alliteration

Ⓑ   Simile

Ⓒ   Metaphor

Ⓓ   Flashback

6   What is the rhyme pattern of each stanza of the poem?

Ⓐ   All the lines rhyme with each other.

Ⓑ   There are two pairs of rhyming lines.

Ⓒ   The second and fourth lines rhyme.

Ⓓ   None of the lines rhyme.

7   Which statement would the poet most likely agree with?

Ⓐ   People should make their own homes like spiders do.

Ⓑ   People should keep their homes free from spider webs.

Ⓒ   People should be aware of the dangers of spiders.

Ⓓ   People should leave spiders alone.

8   The poet states that "to cross your path, he wouldn't dare." What does the phrase "cross your path" refer to?

    Ⓐ   Scaring someone

    Ⓑ   Running into someone

    Ⓒ   Stealing from someone

    Ⓓ   Arguing with someone

9   Which line from the poem uses a metaphor to describe the spider's web?

    Ⓐ   *This small kingdom is his castle,*

    Ⓑ   *He builds his home to be the best.*

    Ⓒ   *His winding, silken web,*

    Ⓓ   *Building homes amongst the darkness,*

10   What does the metaphor identified in Question 9 show?

    Ⓐ   How grand the spider's web is

    Ⓑ   How important the web is to the spider

    Ⓒ   How much detail goes into making the web

    Ⓓ   How hard the spider's web is to spot

STAAR READING

Mini-Test 3

Informational Text

Instructions

This set has one passage for you to read. Read the passage and answer the questions that follow it.

Choose the best answer to each question. Then fill in the circle for the best answer.

To My Teacher

June 15, 2013

Dear Miss Hooper,

I am writing to thank you for the help you have given me this year. We have covered many subjects in class and you have helped me with every single one. You explain things so clearly, and are also amazingly patient. I really believe you have a great skill for teaching others. Without your assistance, I would of struggled to do as well as I have. You should be very proud of the way that you help children to learn. It is because of you that I am thinking about becoming a teacher when I am older.

There were so many highlights this year. Whatever the subject, you made it fun and interesting to everyone. All of your students found learning new things so easy because of you. You never once made me feel silly for asking a question. You were always willing to explain something again and again until I understood. I know you would have explained it a hundred times if that's what it took.

I have mixed feelings about school next year. Firstly, I guess I am sad that you will no longer be my teacher. However, I am pleased that other children will get to share your knowledge. It would be selfish for me to keep you to myself all through school! I hope that they thank you for the good work that you do. You deserve it and it is the least we can do.

I did not enjoy school much before this year. I was new to the school this year. At my old school, I found learning difficult and quite a challenge. It made me so nervous about starting a new school, but the change turned out to be a huge blessing. The last nine months have changed everything. I am now very confident and looking forward to the next school year.

Thank you once again. You have truly been a great teacher and helped me greatly. I hope that we may even share the same classroom again one day.

Yours sincerely,

Jacob Maclean

1   In the sentence below, what does the word <u>highlights</u> refer to?

There were so many highlights this year.

Ⓐ   The best parts

Ⓑ   Challenges

Ⓒ   Breakthroughs

Ⓓ   Main ideas

2   Which sentence from the passage is a fact?

Ⓐ   *Whatever the subject, you made it fun and interesting to everyone.*

Ⓑ   *I really believe you have a great skill for teaching others.*

Ⓒ   *You should be very proud of the way that you help children to learn.*

Ⓓ   *I was new to the school this year.*

3   What is the main reason Jacob wrote the letter?

Ⓐ   To tell how he wants to become a teacher

Ⓑ   To explain that he is leaving the teacher's class

Ⓒ   To express his thanks to his teacher

Ⓓ   To encourage his teacher to keep working hard

4   Which sentence best summarizes the main idea of the letter?

Ⓐ   *It is because of you that I am thinking about becoming a teacher when I am older.*

Ⓑ   *I have mixed feelings about school next year.*

Ⓒ   *I did not enjoy school much before this year.*

Ⓓ   *You have truly been a great teacher and helped me greatly.*

5   In which sentence is Jacob most likely exaggerating Miss Hooper's positive qualities?

Ⓐ   *I really believe you have a great skill for teaching others.*

Ⓑ   *Without your assistance, I would of struggled to do as well as I have.*

Ⓒ   *You never once made me feel silly for asking a question.*

Ⓓ   *I know you would have explained it a hundred times if that's what it took.*

6   How does Jacob feel about not having Miss Hooper as his teacher next year?

Ⓐ   Upset and angry

Ⓑ   Pleased and excited

Ⓒ   Sad, but understanding

Ⓓ   Confused, but unconcerned

7   Which detail best explains why Jacob appreciates Miss Hooper so much?

Ⓐ   After this year, Jacob will not be taught by Miss Hooper.

Ⓑ   Before Miss Hooper, Jacob always found learning difficult.

Ⓒ   During the year, Jacob struggled more than all the other students.

Ⓓ   At his last school, Jacob was bored and made little effort.

8   Which of these is NOT an effect that Miss Hooper had on Jacob?

Ⓐ   Making him look forward to school next year

Ⓑ   Making him want to become a teacher

Ⓒ   Helping him learn more

Ⓓ   Helping him fit in at the new school

9 Look at the chart below.

Why Jacob Thinks Miss Hooper is a Good Teacher

1) She is patient.
2)
3) She makes learning fun.

Which of these best completes the chart?

Ⓐ   She is funny.

Ⓑ   She explains things clearly.

Ⓒ   She gives challenging work.

Ⓓ   She is well-trained.

10 Read this paragraph from the passage.

Thank you once again. You have truly been a great teacher and helped me greatly. I hope that we may even share the same classroom again one day.

How does this paragraph relate to the ideas of the rest of the passage?

Ⓐ   It introduces new ideas.

Ⓑ   It presents evidence against the main ideas.

Ⓒ   It restates the main ideas.

Ⓓ   It gives details to support the main ideas.

STAAR READING

Mini-Test 4

Literary Text

Instructions

This set has one passage for you to read. Read the passage and answer the questions that follow it.

Choose the best answer to each question. Then fill in the circle for the best answer.

The Lighthouse

Simon was fascinated with the lighthouse to the south of the island. It was just two miles from his front door. The lighthouse stood proudly above the sea and cast its light for miles. It had stood in that spot for over two hundred years. Wind and rain had battered it, but the lighthouse stood strong and sturdy. During the day, you could see the aging of the old stone bricks. At night it was an eerie presence. The white stones shone in the moonlight like a ghost hovering over the sea. Simon knew the lighthouse was meant to protect sailors. But sometimes he felt like it was watching him.

Simon often stared at the lighthouse and wondered about its history. He had heard rumors that it was haunted by a stonemason that had helped build it. He had heard how the stonemasons had labored to complete such difficult work by hand. After putting all his effort into building it, one had felt like he could never leave it. He had lived in the lighthouse and later died there. Simon had been told the stonemason's initials were carved into some of the stones. Simon had never been close enough to see it for himself.

One night, Rick was staying at Simon's house. Just like Simon, he couldn't help stare at the lighthouse.

"I think we should head over there," said Rick, who was Simon's best friend. He was always more adventurous than his sensible friend.

Simon thought carefully before responding.

"But aren't you scared?" he asked.

"Not at all. Are you?" Rick replied.

Simon did not want to look scared in front of his best friend.

"No," he replied nervously.

"That is settled then," said Rick. "We will head out this evening."

After dinner, they gathered some food and supplies and packed them into Rick's backpack. Then they headed out toward the lighthouse. Both boys were very quiet as they walked through the fields on the island.

"You're not saying much," said Simon. "Are you okay?"

"I'm fine," said Rick. "I was just thinking."

When they reached the shore, the sun was starting to set above the sea. The boys slowly climbed the small rock face as the sun went down. They both stopped as they stood in front of the lighthouse door.

"In you go then Simon," said Rick, gesturing toward the wooden door.

"You go first," said Simon. "It was your idea."

Rick paused and didn't say a single word. Then Rick edged toward the door. He stopped and looked back at Simon, who gave a small nod of encouragement. He arrived at the step and reached out for the door handle. Simon had stayed back in the shadows. As Rick twisted the handle, he suddenly heard a loud growling from inside.

"Run!" shouted Rick at the top of his voice.

He raced away, with Simon following close behind him. They ran back to the main road and headed back toward Simon's house. Rick looked very sheepish as they made their way home.

"Didn't you want to see inside?" asked Simon.

Rick shrugged and looked down at the ground.

"I guess it was scarier than I thought," he whispered.

"Oh, I don't know," said Simon. "It wasn't that bad."

1   Read this sentence from the passage.

At night it was an eerie presence.

Which word means about the same as <u>eerie</u>?

Ⓐ   Welcoming

Ⓑ   Calming

Ⓒ   Creepy

Ⓓ   Noticeable

2   Which detail given about the lighthouse best explains why it appears frightening?

Ⓐ   It casts its light for miles.

Ⓑ   It was built over two hundred years ago.

Ⓒ   It is made of white stones that seem to shine at night.

Ⓓ   Its job is to protect sailors.

3   Read this sentence from the passage.

Then Rick edged toward the door.

The word <u>edged</u> shows that Rick moved –

Ⓐ   swiftly

Ⓑ   slowly

Ⓒ   suddenly

Ⓓ   smoothly

4   Which statement is most likely true about Rick?

    Ⓐ   He is not scared of anything.

    Ⓑ   He is not as fearless as he says he is.

    Ⓒ   He enjoys seeing how scared Simon is.

    Ⓓ   He only pretends to be frightened.

5   Which word in the sentence below shows that the author is using personification?

> **The lighthouse stood proudly above the sea and cast its light for miles.**

    Ⓐ   *proudly*

    Ⓑ   *above*

    Ⓒ   *light*

    Ⓓ   *miles*

6   Why does Rick tell Simon to run?

    Ⓐ   He sees a creature inside the lighthouse.

    Ⓑ   He hears a noise from inside the lighthouse.

    Ⓒ   He thinks they are going to get in trouble for being inside the lighthouse.

    Ⓓ   He realizes that the owner of the lighthouse is home.

7   What is the point of view in the passage?

Ⓐ   First person

Ⓑ   Second person

Ⓒ   Third person limited

Ⓓ   Third person omniscient

8   According to the passage, how is Simon different from Rick?

Ⓐ   He is more sensible.

Ⓑ   He is more adventurous.

Ⓒ   He is more intelligent.

Ⓓ   He is more determined.

9   Read this sentence from the passage.

Rick shrugged and looked down at the ground.

The author uses this description to suggest that Rick feels –

Ⓐ   angry

Ⓑ   embarrassed

Ⓒ   amused

Ⓓ   terrified

10   How does the old age of the lighthouse help explain why Simon fears it?

Ⓐ   He thinks it may no longer be sturdy.

Ⓑ   He believes it must have special powers to still be standing.

Ⓒ   He has heard that it is haunted by one of the people that built it.

Ⓓ   He worries that it may break down and cause sailors to be harmed.

STAAR READING

Mini-Test 5

Paired Literary Texts

Instructions

This set has two passages for you to read. Read both passages. Then answer the questions about the passages.

Choose the best answer to each question. Then fill in the circle for the best answer.

Directions: Read the next two passages. Then answer the questions.

The Inventor

Scott had always been creative. Ever since he had been a child, he had loved to experiment with new ideas. As Scott had grown, his passion had only grown stronger. After attending university, Scott decided that he wanted to become an inventor. He used his studies in engineering to design and produce many brand new things. His friends thought that he was misguided.

"You cannot spend your life as an inventor," said his best friend Luke. "You will never have a steady income."

Luke worked as a bank manager and worried for his friend's future.

"Why don't you reconsider and get a job in the city?" Luke often asked. "You can always invent on the weekends."

But Scott would not be distracted from his goals.

"This is my dream," he said to Luke. "I have wanted to be an inventor since I was a small child. I am not going to give up."

"But you might spend years trying and never make it," Luke said. "You don't want to look back and realize you wasted all your talent. You're a great engineer, so you know you could get a good job somewhere and do well for yourself."

Scott would explain that he didn't want to work making things that had already been invented. There was no challenge in that. He wanted to use his talents to create something new that would improve how things were done.

"I have to use my talent to do something worthwhile," Scott explained. "I can't waste my time and energy building things that won't make a difference. I have to use all my time wisely."

Luke would shrug and leave his friend to his many different projects. Over several years, Scott developed many ideas that failed to become a success. His first invention was a device that was designed to make a car use less fuel as it traveled. This had many flaws and Scott was unable to sell his invention.

His second idea was a special motorcycle helmet that provided better vision for riders. This invention received little support from people who worked in the industry. Scott's friend Luke continued to encourage him to find a different career.

"Scott, you have to think about your future. I am proud of you for trying so hard to follow your dreams. I think it is now time to try something else. If you don't, I worry about how things will turn out for you."

"Thank you Luke," Scott replied. "I appreciate it. But I cannot stop now. I am so close to coming up with something huge. If I left my designs now, all my life would have been wasted. "

Luke nodded, "I understand my friend. Just know that I am here to support you."

Then one day it happened. Scott completed his design of a new wing for an airplane. It had taken six months. Scott's new invention would improve the efficiency of the plane. He presented it to several companies who all loved his idea. After some competition, a company offered to buy his idea and design plans. Scott accepted the offer.

"I knew that one day I would make it!" he said to Luke as they celebrated.

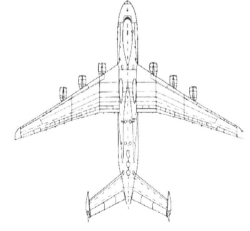

Luke felt a little guilty for ever suggesting that Scott should give up.

"I don't know how you kept going all these years," Luke said. "You definitely deserve every bit of your success."

The Aspiring Star

Troy longed to be a professional basketball player. He had loved the sport ever since he was a small child. He was also very skilled and fast on the basketball court. Despite this, he had one small problem. He was very short. His school coach had suggested that he would never make it in the professional leagues. Although he was devastated at first, he refused to give up on his dream.

Troy had several trials at professional clubs but failed to earn a contract. It was then that he attended the training ground of the Los Angeles Lakers. He asked the coach for a trial. As usual, he was refused. It wasn't in his nature just to walk away.

"But you haven't even given me a chance," said Troy.

"Why should I give you a shot?" asked the coach.

Troy paused before he answered.

"Because one day I am going to be the best player in the world and I will be able to help you out," he replied seriously.

The coach smiled at the confidence of the answer.

"Alright kid," he said. "I'll give you a chance to impress me."

Troy took part in a short practice match and was then allowed to showcase his individual skills. He knew he was being given a rare chance and he put everything he had into it. While the other players took a break for water, Troy stayed on the court and showed even more of his ball skills. He was one of the most skillful players on show and had the will to win to match. The coach was stunned.

"You certainly have a lot of talent for a little fellow," he said. "How would you like to sign on a youth contract?"

Troy agreed and was soon rising through the ranks. He was the shortest player by far, but he was also the hardest worker. He felt he had to work hard to overcome the natural height that he lacked. He practiced his ball skills far longer than everyone else. While he couldn't leap as high as everyone else, he was fast and could dribble the ball around everyone. It was rare to see Troy lose the ball or have it stolen from him. He often stole it from other players, and especially those who underestimated him.

Although some players continued to think he was too short to play, they soon changed their minds when they saw him in action. After two short years, he was a regular for the Lakers and had even won the award as the team's most valuable player. Even with Troy's help, the team was struggling. They were not winning many games and there were rumors that the coach was close to losing his job. It was before a game against the New York Jets that he called Troy into his office for a discussion.

"I have heard that if we lose tonight then I will be replaced as coach," he told Troy. "I need you to do more than play well tonight. I need you to carry the team and win the game. Do you remember your promise before I signed you?"

Troy nodded and smiled at his coach.

"You bet I do coach," he replied. "You bet I do."

Troy went on to play the game of his life that evening. The Lakers won the game and won every game that was left that season. The coach kept his job and led his team on to success.

Directions: Use "The Inventor" to answer the following questions.

1   In the sentence below, which word could best be used in place of <u>flaws</u>?

This had many flaws and Scott was unable to sell his invention.

Ⓐ   Costs

Ⓑ   Faults

Ⓒ   Benefits

Ⓓ   Uses

2   Read this sentence from the passage.

As Scott had grown, his passion had only grown stronger.

The word <u>passion</u> shows that Scott is very –

Ⓐ   enthusiastic

Ⓑ   talented

Ⓒ   impatient

Ⓓ   knowledgeable

3   Which statement best describes how the photograph at the start of the passage relates to the information in the first paragraph?

Ⓐ   It shows how Scott loved to experiment with new ideas.

Ⓑ   It shows how Scott's passion increased as he got older.

Ⓒ   It shows how Scott studied engineering at university.

Ⓓ   It shows how Scott's goals were misguided.

Directions: Use "The Aspiring Star" to answer the following questions.

4   Read this sentence from the passage.

> **Although he was devastated at first, he refused to give up on his dream.**

The word <u>devastated</u> means that Troy was –

Ⓐ   understanding

Ⓑ   very upset

Ⓒ   not surprised

Ⓓ   slightly amused

5   Read this sentence from the passage.

> **I need you to carry the team and win the game.**

What does the phrase "carry the team" refer to?

Ⓐ   How Troy will have to cheer on his teammates

Ⓑ   How Troy will have to do extra work

Ⓒ   How Troy will have to motivate the team

Ⓓ   How Troy will have to go against his team

6   According to the passage, what is the main hurdle that makes it difficult for Troy to play at a high level?

Ⓐ   His talent

Ⓑ   His speed

Ⓒ   His height

Ⓓ   His experience

7 In the third paragraph, Troy asks to be given a chance. How does this affect the rest of the events?

   Ⓐ   It proves to the coach that Troy is fearless enough to do well.

   Ⓑ   It helps Troy understand what it will take to achieve his goal.

   Ⓒ   It encourages the coach to be more open-minded about players.

   Ⓓ   It allows the coach to see how talented Troy is and get a contract.

8 Read this sentence from the end of the passage spoken by the coach.

Do you remember your promise before I signed you?

What promise is the coach referring to?

   Ⓐ   How Troy said he would do anything to win

   Ⓑ   How Troy said he would never leave the team

   Ⓒ   How Troy said he would put his all into every game

   Ⓓ   How Troy said he will help the coach out one day

9 Which statement best explains how you can tell that the point of view is third-person omniscient?

   Ⓐ   The narrator includes dialogue to advance the story.

   Ⓑ   The narrator describes the actions of several characters.

   Ⓒ   The narrator is one of the main characters in the story.

   Ⓓ   The narrator reveals the thoughts of the characters.

Directions: Use both "The Inventor" and "The Aspiring Star" to answer the following questions.

10 Which statement describes a main theme of both passages?

Ⓐ   It is important to keep your promises.

Ⓑ   You can achieve your dreams if you work hard enough.

Ⓒ   A good friend is always there to support you.

Ⓓ   There is no time like the present.

11 Which word best describes both Scott and Troy?

Ⓐ   Foolish

Ⓑ   Determined

Ⓒ   Easygoing

Ⓓ   Sensible

12 Read this dialogue from "The Inventor."

"I have to use my talent to do something worthwhile," Scott explained. "I can't waste my time and energy building things that won't make a difference. I have to use all my time wisely."

Which sentence from "The Aspiring Star" suggests that Troy also believes in using his time wisely?

Ⓐ   *Troy took part in a short practice match and was then allowed to showcase his individual skills.*

Ⓑ   *While the other players took a break for water, Troy stayed on the court and showed even more of his ball skills.*

Ⓒ   *While he couldn't leap as high as everyone else, he was fast and could dribble the ball around everyone.*

Ⓓ   *Although some players continued to think he was too short to play, they soon changed their minds when they saw him in action.*

STAAR READING

Mini-Test 6

Paired Informational Texts

Instructions

This set has two passages for you to read. Read both passages. Then answer the questions about the passages.

Choose the best answer to each question. Then fill in the circle for the best answer.

Directions: Read the next two passages. Then answer the questions.

The Human Skeleton

Did you know that there are over 206 bones in the adult human skeleton? Newborn babies have over 270 bones. As a newborn baby grows, some of their bones are fused together.

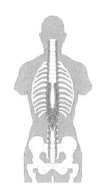

The skeleton performs several very important functions within our body. These include providing a support framework, protecting vital organs, and playing a crucial role in the generation of blood cells. Bones are also a storage site for many of the minerals our bodies need. It is important to keep your bones healthy so they can perform all these roles.

Osteoporosis is a medical condition that occurs when the bones become less dense. This makes them weak and brittle, and can lead to bones fracturing easily. When a bone is very brittle, something as simple as coughing can result in a fracture. Osteoporosis can affect anyone, but is most common in women. Luckily, preventing osteoporosis is quite simple. A diet high in calcium and sufficient exercise will usually prevent osteoporosis.

Three Simple Rules

1. Have a Diet High in Calcium
Your body needs calcium to keep your bones strong. Calcium is found in dairy products, leafy green vegetables, and soy products.

2. Get Enough Vitamin D
Your body uses sunlight to make vitamin D. As long as you spend a normal amount of time outdoors, your body should be getting enough vitamin D. Vitamin D is also found in salmon, tuna, and eggs.

3. Exercise
Regular exercise will keep your bones strong and healthy. Walking, running, jogging, or playing sports are all good for the health of your bones.

Food Poisoning

Bacteria grow quickly in the right conditions. When food isn't prepared, kept, or handled properly it has the potential to make you very ill. Food poisoning occurs when bacteria are introduced into food before it is eaten. Food poisoning can sometimes be as mild as having a stomachache, but it can also be much more serious. The Centers for Disease Control and Prevention (CDC) states that almost 50 million Americans get food poisoning every year. Of those, around 125,000 people are admitted to hospital and there are around 3,000 deaths. Luckily, food poisoning can be prevented. All you have to do is follow a few simple rules.

1: Wash your hands and the equipment you're going to use to prepare and serve the food.

2: Don't use the same chopping board for meat that you use to prepare fruit and vegetables. This is especially important if the fruit and vegetables are served raw.

3: Ensure your food is cooked thoroughly. The cooking process destroys most harmful bacteria, so this step can prevent food poisoning even when the raw food contains bacteria.

4: Properly store your food.

5: Make sure your refrigerator temperature is set low enough.

6: Follow the directions on packaging for how to store foods once they are open, and for how long to store food for.

7: Don't unfreeze and then refreeze food.

Top Tip

Many foods have to be used within a few days once they've been opened. It can be easy to forget when something was opened. Keep a marker near the fridge and write on the packaging what date the food was opened.

Directions: Use "The Human Skeleton" to answer the following questions.

1   Which two words from the passage have about the same meaning?

    Ⓐ   *storage, minerals*

    Ⓑ   *sunlight, outdoors*

    Ⓒ   *adult, newborn*

    Ⓓ   *vital, crucial*

2   Which of the following should NOT be added to the web?

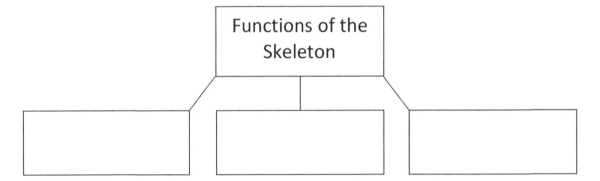

    Ⓐ   being a support framework

    Ⓑ   protecting the organs

    Ⓒ   storing minerals

    Ⓓ   preventing illness

3 According to the passage, how are adults different from children?

Ⓐ They have more bones.

Ⓑ They have fewer bones.

Ⓒ Their bones have more purposes.

Ⓓ Their bones have fewer purposes.

4 What is the main reason the author begins the passage with a question?

Ⓐ To present a fact in a way that creates interest in the topic

Ⓑ To explain the main purpose of the article

Ⓒ To suggest that many people do not realize the importance of the skeleton

Ⓓ To encourage readers to research and find out more about the human skeleton

5 The passage states that the skeleton plays a role in the generation of blood cells. What does the word generation most likely refer to?

Ⓐ Making blood cells

Ⓑ Protecting blood cells

Ⓒ Repairing blood cells

Ⓓ Checking on blood cells

Directions: Use "Food Poisoning" to answer the following questions.

6   In rule 3, which word could best be used in place of <u>thoroughly</u>?

    Ⓐ   Quickly

    Ⓑ   Completely

    Ⓒ   Cleanly

    Ⓓ   Nicely

7   Which rule does the information in the box mainly relate to?

    Ⓐ   Rule 1

    Ⓑ   Rule 3

    Ⓒ   Rule 5

    Ⓓ   Rule 6

8   What is the main purpose of the first paragraph?

    Ⓐ   To describe how to prevent food poisoning

    Ⓑ   To explain the importance of food safety

    Ⓒ   To encourage people to cook their own food

    Ⓓ   To show that bacteria can grow anywhere

9   Which of these rules from the passage best supports the conclusion that bacteria grow poorly in cold conditions?

    Ⓐ   *Don't use the same chopping board for chopping meat that you use to prepare fruit and vegetables.*

    Ⓑ   *Ensure your food is cooked thoroughly.*

    Ⓒ   *Make sure your refrigerator temperature is set low enough.*

    Ⓓ   *Don't unfreeze and then refreeze food.*

Directions: Use both "The Human Skeleton" and "Food Poisoning" to answer the following questions.

10   Which of these ideas is found in both passages?

    Ⓐ   Health problems can be avoided by making the right decisions.

    Ⓑ   Each system of the body plays more than one role in good health.

    Ⓒ   Fresh fruit and vegetables are a key factor in staying healthy.

    Ⓓ   It is harder for adults to stay in good health than it is for children.

11   Which of these describes a main purpose of both passages?

    Ⓐ   Explaining the role that bacteria play in disease

    Ⓑ   Persuading people to have a balanced diet

    Ⓒ   Giving advice on how to prevent a health problem

    Ⓓ   Encouraging people to prepare food carefully

12   Data given in each passage is shown below.

> **Did you know that there are over 206 bones in the adult human skeleton? Newborn babies have over 270 bones.**
>
> **The Centers for Disease Control and Prevention (CDC) states that almost 50 million Americans get food poisoning every year. Of those, around 125,000 people are admitted to hospital and there are around 3,000 deaths.**

Compared to the data in "The Human Skeleton," the data in "Food Poisoning" creates a sense of –

    Ⓐ   seriousness

    Ⓑ   curiosity

    Ⓒ   doubt

    Ⓓ   surprise

Section 2: Vocabulary Quizzes

INTRODUCTION TO THE VOCABULARY QUIZZES
For Parents, Teachers, and Tutors

How Vocabulary is Assessed by the State of Texas

The STAAR Reading test includes multiple-choice questions that assess vocabulary skills. These questions follow each passage and are mixed in with the reading comprehension questions.

These questions require students to complete the following tasks:
- use context to determine the meaning of unfamiliar words
- use context to determine the meaning of multiple meaning words
- determine the meaning of words with suffixes
- determine the meaning of words with prefixes
- determine the meaning of words derived from Latin and Greek roots or affixes
- use a dictionary, glossary, or thesaurus to determine word meaning, syllabication, pronunciation, alternate word choices, and parts of speech

About the Vocabulary Quizzes

This section of the practice test book contains six quizzes. Each quiz tests one vocabulary skill that is covered on the state test.

This section of the book covers all of the vocabulary skills assessed on the STAAR Reading test. The aim of the quizzes is to help ensure that students have all the vocabulary skills that they will need for the STAAR Reading test. If students can master this section of the book, they will be ready to answer the vocabulary questions.

Quiz 1: Use Context to Determine Word Meaning

1 What does the word <u>barely</u> mean in the sentence below?

The cave was so dark that Ken could barely see anything.

Ⓐ Only

Ⓑ Hardly

Ⓒ Empty

Ⓓ Scary

2 What does the word <u>peculiar</u> mean in the sentence below?

Tia worried because Joy had been acting peculiar all week.

Ⓐ Odd

Ⓑ Mean

Ⓒ Normal

Ⓓ Friendly

3 If a situation is described as <u>grim</u>, it is —

Ⓐ quite unusual

Ⓑ easily fixed

Ⓒ odd and amusing

Ⓓ very serious

4   What does the word <u>gale</u> in the sentence below show?

Chloe had expected a storm, but not such a gale.

   Ⓐ   The storm was over quickly.

   Ⓑ   The storm lasted a long time.

   Ⓒ   There was a lot of rain.

   Ⓓ   There were strong winds.

5   What does the word <u>furious</u> mean in the sentence below?

I was furious when I found out my computer was broken.

   Ⓐ   Worried

   Ⓑ   Surprised

   Ⓒ   Angry

   Ⓓ   Puzzled

6   What does the word <u>produce</u> mean?

The factory could produce thousands of items each day.

   Ⓐ   Find

   Ⓑ   Make

   Ⓒ   Lose

   Ⓓ   Sell

7 Why does the author use the word <u>snapped</u> in the sentence?

Miss Rivera snapped and started yelling.

Ⓐ   To show that Miss Rivera yelled loudly

Ⓑ   To show that Miss Rivera became angry suddenly

Ⓒ   To show that Miss Rivera hurt herself

Ⓓ   To show that Miss Rivera took action

8 Read the sentence below.

The water trickled down the rocks.

Which word is closest in meaning to <u>trickled</u>?

Ⓐ   Rushed

Ⓑ   Flooded

Ⓒ   Dripped

Ⓓ   Wandered

9 What does the word <u>circular</u> describe about the table?

The oak table was smooth, heavy, and circular.

Ⓐ   What it is made of

Ⓑ   What it is used for

Ⓒ   What it feels like

Ⓓ   What shape it is

Quiz 2: Understand and Use Multiple Meaning Words

1 What does the word <u>block</u> mean in the sentence below?

> **Wayne asked if the trash was going to block the path.**

Ⓐ   A group of buildings

Ⓑ   A solid piece of something

Ⓒ   To be in the way

Ⓓ   To join something to wood

2 In which sentence does <u>right</u> mean the same as below?

> **Chelsea helped because it was the right thing to do.**

Ⓐ   I drove to the end of the street and turned right.

Ⓑ   James said that we should leave right away.

Ⓒ   The right to free speech is an important idea.

Ⓓ   Stella always tries to do what is right.

3 What does the word <u>rock</u> mean in the sentence?

> **The grandmother liked to rock the baby to sleep.**

Ⓐ   A pebble or stone

Ⓑ   To affect someone greatly

Ⓒ   To move from side to side

Ⓓ   A type of music

4 How is <u>hurling</u> an object different from <u>throwing</u> it?

    Ⓐ   The object is thrown straight up.

    Ⓑ   The object is thrown with force.

    Ⓒ   The object is thrown lightly.

    Ⓓ   The object is small and light.

5 In which sentence does <u>jam</u> mean the same as below?

Connor tried to jam all the clothes into the bag.

    Ⓐ   The photocopier beeped because it had a jam.

    Ⓑ   Joy was late to work because of a traffic jam.

    Ⓒ   Kimmy had to jam on the brakes to stop in time.

    Ⓓ   Steve couldn't jam the sleeping bag back into its case.

6 Why does the author use the word <u>rushed</u> in the sentence?

The water rushed down the mountain stream.

    Ⓐ   To show that the water sounded loud

    Ⓑ   To show that the water moved quickly

    Ⓒ   To show that the water was clear

    Ⓓ   To show that there was only a little water

Quiz 3: Understand and Use Prefixes

1   What does the word <u>preheat</u> mean?

    Ⓐ   Heat more

    Ⓑ   Not heat

    Ⓒ   Heat before

    Ⓓ   Heat again

2   Which prefix is added to <u>print</u> to make a word meaning "print wrongly"?

    Ⓐ   pre-

    Ⓑ   non-

    Ⓒ   mis-

    Ⓓ   un-

3   Which prefix should be added to the word to make the sentence correct?

Miss Kim ___abled the alarm so she could enter her home.

    Ⓐ   un-

    Ⓑ   dis-

    Ⓒ   in-

    Ⓓ   mis-

4   What does the substance <u>antifreeze</u> most likely do?

    Ⓐ   Make something freeze quicker

    Ⓑ   Stop something from freezing

    Ⓒ   Check to see if something will freeze

    Ⓓ   Freeze something many times

5   Which prefix can be added to the word <u>just</u> to make a word meaning "not just"?

Ⓐ   un-

Ⓑ   in-

Ⓒ   mis-

Ⓓ   dis-

6   Which word contains the prefix <u>re-</u>?

Ⓐ   Recipe

Ⓑ   Rewrite

Ⓒ   Reading

Ⓓ   Reason

7   If a person's desk is <u>disorganized</u>, it is –

Ⓐ   new

Ⓑ   messy

Ⓒ   empty

Ⓓ   heavy

8   Which word means "perform better than"?

Ⓐ   Underperform

Ⓑ   Misperform

Ⓒ   Reperform

Ⓓ   Outperform

Quiz 4: Understand and Use Suffixes

1 What does the word <u>keenest</u> mean?

   Ⓐ   Not keen

   Ⓑ   More keen

   Ⓒ   The most keen

   Ⓓ   In a way that is keen

2 Which suffix can be added to the word <u>meaning</u> to make a word meaning "without meaning"?

   Ⓐ   -less

   Ⓑ   -ful

   Ⓒ   -ness

   Ⓓ   -ly

3 Which word means "a state of being damp"?

   Ⓐ   Damper

   Ⓑ   Dampen

   Ⓒ   Dampness

   Ⓓ   Damply

4 If a person's actions are described as <u>predictable</u>, the actions –

   Ⓐ   are being talked about

   Ⓑ   have not happened before

   Ⓒ   are unusual

   Ⓓ   can be guessed

5   Which suffix should be added to the word to make the sentence correct?

Samuel kind__ asked Sarah if she needed any help.

Ⓐ   -ly

Ⓑ   -est

Ⓒ   -ness

Ⓓ   -er

6   What does the word <u>plentiful</u> mean?

Ⓐ   Having plenty

Ⓑ   Less plenty

Ⓒ   More plenty

Ⓓ   Not plenty

7   Which suffix can be added to the word <u>weed</u> to make a word meaning "full of weeds"?

Ⓐ   -ness

Ⓑ   -ing

Ⓒ   -y

Ⓓ   -ed

8   In which word is the suffix <u>-est</u> used?

Ⓐ   Retest

Ⓑ   Chest

Ⓒ   Driest

Ⓓ   Guest

Quiz 5: Use Greek and Latin Roots

1   The word <u>biology</u> contains the Greek root <u>bio-</u>. <u>Biology</u> is probably the study of –

   Ⓐ   life

   Ⓑ   water

   Ⓒ   books

   Ⓓ   people

2   The Latin root <u>jus-</u> is used in the word <u>justice</u>. What does the Latin root <u>jus-</u> mean?

   Ⓐ   Problem

   Ⓑ   Proof

   Ⓒ   Law

   Ⓓ   Person

3   The word <u>periscope</u> is based on the Greek roots <u>peri-</u> and <u>scop-</u>, which mean "around" and "look at." Based on this, what is a <u>periscope</u>?

   Ⓐ   A tool for measuring distance

   Ⓑ   A tool that is easy to find

   Ⓒ   A tool for seeing many different ways

   Ⓓ   A tool that has been studied

4   The word <u>centenary</u> contains the Latin root <u>cent-</u>. If a library is celebrating its <u>centenary</u>, it is –

Ⓐ   two years old

Ⓑ   ten years old

Ⓒ   one hundred years old

Ⓓ   one thousand years old

5   The Latin root <u>flor-</u> is used in the word <u>floral</u>. What does the Latin root <u>flor-</u> mean?

Ⓐ   Yellow

Ⓑ   Tiny

Ⓒ   Smell

Ⓓ   Flower

6   The word <u>exoskeleton</u> is based on the Greek root <u>exo-</u>. Based on this, what does <u>exoskeleton</u> mean?

Ⓐ   A skeleton that is on the outside

Ⓑ   A skeleton that is strong

Ⓒ   A skeleton that is inside

Ⓓ   A skeleton that is large

7   The word <u>audible</u> contains the Latin root <u>aud-</u>. The word <u>audible</u> means that something can be –

Ⓐ   seen

Ⓑ   tasted

Ⓒ   heard

Ⓓ   touched

Quiz 6: Use a Dictionary, Glossary, or Thesaurus

1 What is the correct way to divide <u>delicate</u> into syllables?

   Ⓐ   del-i-cate

   Ⓑ   delic-ate

   Ⓒ   de-li-cate

   Ⓓ   de-lic-ate

2 Read this thesaurus entry for the word <u>blunder</u>.

> **blunder** *noun*
> blooper, botch, bungle, error, fault, mistake

What is the purpose of the list of words?

   Ⓐ   To show the different meanings the word can have

   Ⓑ   To give words with about the same meaning

   Ⓒ   To explain the exact meaning of the word

   Ⓓ   To show how the word came to be used

3 Read this dictionary entry for the word <u>blizzard</u>.

> **blizzard** [bliz-erd]
> *noun*
> 1. a storm with dry snow, strong winds, and cold temperatures

What does "[bliz-erd]" in the entry explain?

   Ⓐ   What the word means

   Ⓑ   What type of word it is

   Ⓒ   How to say the word

   Ⓓ   Where the word comes from

4 Read this dictionary entry for the word <u>dense</u>.

> **dense** *adjective*
> 1. crowded or grouped closely together 2. not intelligent
> 3. only letting a little light through 4. difficult to understand

Which definition of the word <u>dense</u> is used in the sentence below?

Frank struggled to push his bike through the dense grass.

Ⓐ   Definition 1

Ⓑ   Definition 2

Ⓒ   Definition 3

Ⓓ   Definition 4

5 Read this dictionary entry for the word <u>kid</u>.

> **kid**
> *noun*
> 1. a young goat 2. (informal) a young person or child
> *verb*
> 3. to tease or make fun of 4. to lie in a joking way

Which definition of the word <u>kid</u> is used in the sentence below?

"Is that the new kid that moved here from Miami?" Raymond asked his friend as they took their seats on the school bus.

Ⓐ   Definition 1

Ⓑ   Definition 2

Ⓒ   Definition 3

Ⓓ   Definition 4

Section 3: Reading Practice Test 1

INTRODUCTION TO THE READING PRACTICE TEST
For Parents, Teachers, and Tutors

How Reading is Assessed by the State of Texas

The STAAR Reading test assesses reading skills by having students read literary and informational passages and answer questions about the passages. On the actual STAAR test, students will read 4 or 5 individual passages, as well as 1 or 2 sets of paired passages. Students will answer a total of 44 multiple-choice questions.

About the STAAR Reading Practice Test

This section of the book contains a practice test similar to the real STAAR Reading test. To ensure that all skills are tested, it is slightly longer than the real test. It has 5 individual passages, 1 set of paired passages, and a total of 54 questions. The questions cover all the skills tested on the STAAR Reading test, and have the same formats.

Taking the Test

Students are given 4 hours to complete the actual STAAR Reading test. Individual schools are allowed to determine their own schedule, though the test must be completed on the same school day. Schools may choose to include breaks or to complete the test in two or more sessions.

This practice test is designed to be taken in two sessions of 2 hours each. You can use the same time limit, or you can choose not to time the test. In real testing situations, students will complete the two sessions on the same day. You can follow this schedule, or you can choose your own schedule.

Students complete the STAAR Reading test by marking their answers on an answer sheet. An answer sheet is included in the back of the book.

Reading Skills

The STAAR Reading test assesses a specific set of skills. These skills are described in the TEKS, or Texas Essential Knowledge and Skills. The full answer key at the end of the book identifies the specific skill that each question is testing.

STAAR Reading

Practice Test 1

Session 1

Instructions
Read the passages. Each passage is followed by questions.
Read each question carefully. Then select the best answer. Fill in the circle for the best answer.

Mark Zuckerberg

Mark Zuckerberg is a web site developer and computer programmer. He is also a businessperson. He is best known for creating the web site Facebook. Facebook is a web site that allows people to connect with friends and family. He is now the CEO and president of the company.

Zuckerberg founded the web site in 2004 with some of his Harvard University classmates. He has since overseen the development of the site. Facebook became the most visited online web site throughout 2010. This was also the year that Mark Zuckerberg was named as Person of the Year by *Time Magazine*.

Mark Zuckerberg was born in White Plains, New York in 1984. His early education was spent at Ardsley High School. This was followed by Phillips Exeter Academy. While at Phillips Exeter Academy, he won prizes for his work in science, mathematics, astronomy, and physics. His outdoor pursuits included fencing, and he was captain of the college fencing team. He is also multilingual and can speak French, Latin, Hebrew, and Ancient Greek.

Zuckerberg first showed an interest in computers during middle school. At this time, he started to write software programs. His father hired an experienced software developer, David Newman, to tutor his son. He was identified at this young age to be an amazing talent. This encouraged him to take a graduate course in software design while at high school. He continued to develop computer programs as he learned.

Zuckerberg's main interest was in software that helped people to interact and communicate. This passion inspired a program called ZuckNet. This allowed a small set of users to communicate by 'pinging' each other. It was like a basic version of today's instant messenger tools. Zuckerberg continued to experiment with different software programs. Then he enrolled at Harvard University. During this time, he focused on creating software that connected people through common interests. The inspiration for Facebook came from paper-based books at the university. The books were known as facebooks and showed students' names, photographs, and gave information about them.

Facebook was launched on February 4, 2004. At first it was only for Harvard University students. It soon spread to other major universities including Stanford, Columbia, Yale, and MIT. This was followed by a spread to most universities in the United States. In 2005, it was made available to high schools. This was followed by allowing people from large companies like Apple and Microsoft to join. In 2006, it was made available to anyone over the age of 13. The site has grown rapidly since then. In 2012, Facebook had over one billion users worldwide.

On May 18, 2012, Facebook took another major step in its history. It listed on the stock exchange. It was one of the biggest listings in history. On the day of its listing, Facebook had a total value of just over $100 billion. Mark Zuckerberg was given the honor of ringing the bell to open stock market trading on the day. He rang the bell from the Facebook campus in California surrounded by cheering staff.

The site continues to grow and change. As of January 2014, Zuckerberg remains as chairman and CEO of Facebook, and has an estimated total wealth of just over $25 billion. In 2010, he pledged to give at least half of his wealth to charity over his lifetime. His donations have included giving over $100 million to public schools in New Jersey, supporting various small Internet businesses, and giving almost $1 billion worth of Facebook shares to the Silicon Valley Community Foundation.

One other thing Mark Zuckerberg is known for is wearing hoodies. While a suit and tie is the expected choice for a business meeting, he appears at many wearing a hoodie and slide-on sandals. This kind of casual clothing is also usually his choice for presentations and other public events. Some have said that his style of dress shows his lack of seriousness. Others argue that he values what he does above what he looks like.

© Elaine Chan and Priscilla Chan, Wikimedia Commons

1   As it is used in the sentence, what does the word <u>common</u> mean?

During this time, he focused on creating software that connected people through common interests.

Ⓐ   Ordinary

Ⓑ   Everyday

Ⓒ   Shared

Ⓓ   General

2   What does the prefix in the word <u>multilingual</u> mean?

He is also multilingual and can speak French, Latin, Hebrew, and Ancient Greek.

Ⓐ   Many

Ⓑ   Early

Ⓒ   One

Ⓓ   Language

3   According to the passage, which of these groups were the first to be allowed to join Facebook?

Ⓐ   University students

Ⓑ   Employees of large companies

Ⓒ   High school students

Ⓓ   Harvard University professors

4 Which paragraph has the main purpose of describing how Zuckerberg first developed his computer skills?

Ⓐ   Paragraph 1

Ⓑ   Paragraph 2

Ⓒ   Paragraph 3

Ⓓ   Paragraph 4

5 Which sentence from the passage best shows that Facebook is successful?

Ⓐ   *Facebook is a web site that allows people to connect with friends and family.*

Ⓑ   *Facebook became the most visited online web site throughout 2010.*

Ⓒ   *Facebook was launched on February 4, 2004.*

Ⓓ   *This was followed by allowing people from large companies like Apple and Microsoft to join.*

6 Why did Mark Zuckerberg's father most likely hire a software developer to tutor his son?

Ⓐ   He was worried that Mark was making mistakes.

Ⓑ   He saw that Mark had a talent worth developing.

Ⓒ   He saw that Mark was struggling with his studies.

Ⓓ   He wanted Mark to develop useful programs.

7 This passage is most like –

Ⓐ   a biography

Ⓑ   an autobiography

Ⓒ   a short story

Ⓓ   a news article

8 The web below summarizes information from the passage.

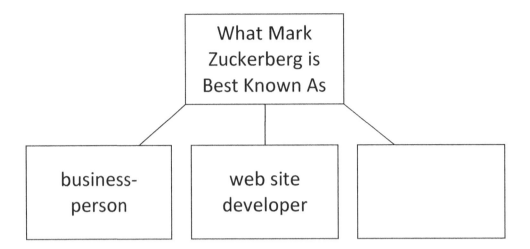

Which of these best completes the web?

Ⓐ teacher

Ⓑ college professor

Ⓒ computer programmer

Ⓓ fencing champion

9 What does the photograph and the caption show about Zuckerberg's personality?

Ⓐ He is independent and doesn't always do what others expect.

Ⓑ He is humble and doesn't want others to know of his success.

Ⓒ He is busy and doesn't have time to organize his life properly.

Ⓓ He is selfish and doesn't think about how he affects others.

Tara's Fear

Tara was scared of flying. She always had been ever since she was a little girl. It hadn't been a problem for her as a child though, as her parents never took a vacation overseas. Despite this, Tara's fear grew steadily the older she got. She hated the idea of being up in the air and in flight.

One year her family announced that they would take their vacation abroad. They were going to New Zealand. Her father had planned an adventure trip that included white water rafting, fly fishing, and trekking up an old volcano. Tara had just turned 13 years old. Everything her father described sounded like the kind of great adventure she had only read about in books. She was excited by the thought of it all, but she couldn't stop thinking about the long flight there. She longed to go, but she didn't know if she could cope with the flight there. She was so distraught that she finally claimed that she simply could not go. As she lay crying on her bed at the thought, her father walked into her room.

"I can't do it, Dad," she said sobbing. "I won't be able to fly."

Her father placed his hand gently on her shoulder.

"I know honey," he whispered. "It's really difficult for you. I know exactly how you feel."

Tara looked up at her father. "Do you really?" she asked.

"When I was your age, I had a phobia too," he replied. "I never thought I'd ever get over it."

Tara sat upright on the bed. She would never have guessed that her father could be scared of anything.

"What were you scared of Dad?" she asked.

Her father looked at her before replying.

"It seems silly now, but I used to be scared of spiders. Whenever I saw one I would scream and run in the other direction. When I was young, I didn't even like playing outside because of spiders and small insects. One year my mother told me that we were going camping. I immediately refused to go. The idea of sleeping under the stars with all of those bugs scared the life out of me!"

"What happened then, Dad?" asked Tara.

"Well my mother talked to me," he replied. "She explained that she understood why I was scared, but that it was something that she could help me to overcome. Then she told me that once I did get over my fear, I would be able to enjoy being outdoors much more. She made me realize that I couldn't let a spider stop me from ever enjoying being outdoors. I had to focus on all the fun I would be having, not on the one thing that scared me."

A small smile crept across Tara's face.

"So did you go in the end then, Dad?" she asked.

"You bet I did," he replied without hesitation. "It was a challenge, but I kept thinking about my mother's words. They inspired me to face my fears. I went camping with my family and had the time of my life. You'll have the time of your life on our trip. You can't let your fear of the plane stop you from having all those good times. You just close your eyes and imagine yourself in New Zealand and don't let your fear take the good times away from you."

Tara suddenly felt determined. She was going to stand up to her fear and not let it steal her trip from her.

"Thanks Dad," said Tara. "You'd better make sure you book me a seat on the plane because I'm coming whether my fear likes it or not."

10 What does the word <u>distraught</u> mean in the sentence below?

She was so distraught that she finally claimed that she simply could not go.

Ⓐ Disbelieving

Ⓑ Distressed

Ⓒ Uncertain

Ⓓ Determined

11 In the sentence below, which word means about the same as <u>steadily</u>?

Despite this, Tara's fear grew steadily the older she got.

Ⓐ Swiftly

Ⓑ Weirdly

Ⓒ Suddenly

Ⓓ Gradually

12 How does Tara feel when her father first says that he had a phobia?

Ⓐ Alarmed

Ⓑ Surprised

Ⓒ Excited

Ⓓ Relieved

13   Why does Tara have mixed feelings about the trip to New Zealand?

    Ⓐ   She thinks the activities planned will be exciting, but also worries that they will be dangerous.

    Ⓑ   She wants to go to New Zealand, but is afraid of the long flight to get there.

    Ⓒ   She knows that her father will be there to support her, but worries that she might ruin his trip.

    Ⓓ   She wants to enjoy her time in New Zealand, but she is scared of being so far from home.

14   Read this sentence spoken by the father.

The idea of sleeping under the stars with all of those bugs scared the life out of me!

Which literary device does the father use to emphasize how fearful he felt?

    Ⓐ   Imagery, using details to create an image or picture

    Ⓑ   Hyperbole, using exaggeration to make a point

    Ⓒ   Simile, comparing two items using the words "like" or "as"

    Ⓓ   Symbolism, using an object to stand for something else

15   Which statement best describes how you can tell that the passage is realistic fiction?

    Ⓐ   It has a theme that can be applied in real life.

    Ⓑ   It describes events that could really happen.

    Ⓒ   It has a modern setting.

    Ⓓ   It has a main problem.

16 Which statement best explains how the father's past experiences allows him to help his daughter?

Ⓐ His description of overcoming his fears inspires Tara to feel like she can be braver.

Ⓑ His experience facing his own fears shows Tara that there is really nothing to be afraid of.

Ⓒ His story about being afraid of spiders makes Tara realize how silly her fears are.

Ⓓ His account of having to miss out on things makes Tara feel bad about making her father miss the trip.

17 How are Tara and Tara's father similar?

Ⓐ They have the same fear of flying.

Ⓑ They have never flown before.

Ⓒ They receive help to overcome a fear from a parent.

Ⓓ They are thoughtful and understanding.

18 The main theme of the passage is about –

Ⓐ admitting your fears

Ⓑ letting other people help you

Ⓒ not letting your fears hold you back

Ⓓ making the most of every opportunity

Manchester United Soccer Club

About Soccer

1. Soccer is a ball sport that was invented in England in the 1800s. It is an outdoor sport. An individual match sees two teams of 11 players compete against each other. The object of the game is to work the ball into one of the two goals positioned at each end of the field.

2. It is a sport that is played all over the world. It is most popular in South America and Europe. The most successful international team is Brazil. They have won five World Cups since 1930, which is a competition that is held every 4 years. Italy has won four World Cups. Germany is not far behind, with three wins.

3. Soccer is not as popular as sports like baseball and football in the United States. The 2013 championship match of Major League Soccer in America had a crowd of 21,650. This is much less than for the Super Bowl, which had 71,000 people. However, soccer is a very entertaining sport to watch. Soccer may become a favorite sport in the United States one day.

4. As with popular American sports, major teams enjoy the massive support of their fans. Manchester United Soccer Club is based in the United Kingdom and is one of the most-loved teams. The love that fans have of the team is based on their long history, their success, and the talented and popular players that have been part of the team.

A Famous Soccer Club

5. Manchester United is a famous soccer team. They are based in the United Kingdom. They play in the English Premier League and the European Champions League. They are known as one of the most successful soccer clubs in the world.

6.   They were first formed in 1888. At this time, they were named the Newton Heath Football Club. In 1901, they were sold and were given the new name of Manchester United.

7.   They are the most successful club in the English League. They have won the English Premier League nineteen times. This is one more than their nearest rivals, Liverpool.

8.   Since 1958, Manchester United have also won the European Champions League three times. This competition features teams from across Europe. It is this success that has helped them become such a well-known team.

9.   David Beckham is one of the club's most famous players. He played for Manchester United from 1993 until 2003. In this time, he scored 62 goals for the club and helped his team win eight championships. He scored some amazing goals, including one from the halfway line that floated above the goalkeeper's head and curved into the net. The goal became so famous that it was voted by the British public as number 18 on a list of 100 greatest sporting moments. Beckham was known for being able to curve or bend the ball. It allowed him to score some amazing goals. These thrilled fans and helped draw huge crowds to games.

©Wikimedia Commons

10. In 2007, Beckham made an unexpected move. He joined America's Major League Soccer, and began playing for Los Angeles Galaxy. He was paid around $6.5 million per year. One of the most interesting things about the deal was that Beckham was not just paid by the Los Angeles Galaxy team. He was also paid by all the teams in America's Major League Soccer. The teams agreed to this because they hoped that having such a major star in their league would attract more people to the sport.

Manchester United's English Premier League Grand Final Wins

Year	Team Defeated
1908	Aston Villa
1911	Aston Villa
1952	Tottenham
1956	Blackpool
1957	Tottenham
1965	Leeds United
1967	Nottingham Forest
1993	Aston Villa
1994	Blackburn Rovers
1996	Newcastle United
1997	Newcastle United
1999	Arsenal
2000	Arsenal
2001	Arsenal
2003	Arsenal
2007	Chelsea
2008	Chelsea
2009	Chelsea
2011	Chelsea

19   Which meaning of the word <u>object</u> is used in the sentence below?

The object of the game is to work the ball into one of the two goals positioned at each end of the field.

Ⓐ   A goal or aim

Ⓑ   A type of item

Ⓒ   To argue against

Ⓓ   To refuse to do something

20   Where was the game of soccer invented?

Ⓐ   England

Ⓑ   Brazil

Ⓒ   Italy

Ⓓ   Germany

21   Which sentence from paragraph 3 uses a comparison to support the main claim below?

Soccer is not as popular as sports like baseball and football in the United States.

Ⓐ   *The 2013 championship match of Major League Soccer in America had a crowd of 21,650.*

Ⓑ   *This is much less than for the Super Bowl, which had 71,000 people.*

Ⓒ   *However, soccer is a very entertaining sport to watch.*

Ⓓ   *Soccer may become a favorite sport in the United States one day.*

22   Which sentence is best supported by the information in the table at the end of the passage?

(A)   *They have won the English Premier League nineteen times.*

(B)   *This is one more than their nearest rivals, Liverpool.*

(C)   *Since 1958, Manchester United have also won the European Champions League three times.*

(D)   *This competition features teams from across Europe.*

23   Which sentence gives an opinion on Manchester United?

(A)   *They are based in the United Kingdom.*

(B)   *In 1901, they were sold and were given the new name of Manchester United.*

(C)   *Since 1958, Manchester United have also won the European Champions League three times.*

(D)   *It is this success that has helped them become such a well-known team.*

24   Paragraph 10 describes how David Beckham was paid by all the teams in America's Major League Soccer. Which idea from "About Soccer" does this detail best support?

(A)   Soccer is played all over the world.

(B)   Soccer is not as popular in America as other sports.

(C)   Soccer teams in Europe enjoy massive support from their fans.

(D)   Soccer is played by teams of 11 players.

25 Which team has been defeated by Manchester United in the English Premier League final exactly three times?

Ⓐ Aston Villa

Ⓑ Tottenham

Ⓒ Newcastle United

Ⓓ Chelsea

26 What is the main purpose of the seventh and eighth paragraphs?

Ⓐ To describe how the team formed

Ⓑ To describe the team's achievements

Ⓒ To explain why the team is successful

Ⓓ To show that the team has improved over time

27 Read this dictionary entry for the word deal.

> **deal** *noun*
> 1. a business agreement 2. a bargain 3. the treatment given to somebody 4. the distribution of cards

Now read this sentence from the passage.

> **One of the most interesting things about the deal was that Beckham was not just paid by the Los Angeles Galaxy team.**

Which definition of the word deal is used in the sentence above?

Ⓐ Definition 1

Ⓑ Definition 2

Ⓒ Definition 3

Ⓓ Definition 4

END OF SESSION 1

STAAR Reading

Practice Test 1

Session 2

Instructions

Read the passages. Each passage is followed by questions.

Read each question carefully. Then select the best answer. Fill in the circle for the best answer.

Little White Lily
By George Macdonald

1   Little White Lily
Sat by a stone,
Drooping and waiting
Till the sun shone.

2   Little White Lily
Sunshine has fed;
Little White Lily
Is lifting her head.

3   Little White Lily
Said: "It is good
Little White Lily's
Clothing and food."

4   Little White Lily
Dressed like a bride!
Shining with whiteness,
And crowned beside!

5   Little White Lily
Drooping with pain,
Waiting and waiting
For the wet rain.

6   Little White Lily
Holdeth her cup;
Rain is fast falling
And filling it up.

7   Little White Lily
Said: "Good again,
When I am thirsty
To have the nice rain.

8   Now I am stronger,
Now I am cool;
Heat cannot burn me,
My veins are so full."

9   Little White Lily
Smells very sweet;
On her head sunshine,
Rain at her feet.

10   Thanks to the sunshine,
Thanks to the rain,
Little White Lily
Is happy again.

28   Based on the poem, what is most important to the lily?

Ⓐ   Having water

Ⓑ   Smelling nice

Ⓒ   Being appreciated

Ⓓ   Getting shelter

29   What is the rhyme pattern of each stanza of the poem?

Ⓐ   The second and fourth lines rhyme.

Ⓑ   There are two pairs of rhyming lines.

Ⓒ   The first and last lines rhyme.

Ⓓ   None of the lines rhyme.

30   Which line from the poem contains alliteration?

Ⓐ   *Drooping and waiting*

Ⓑ   *Sunshine has fed;*

Ⓒ   *Shining with whiteness,*

Ⓓ   *Rain is fast falling*

31   Which of the following is used throughout the poem?

Ⓐ   Symbolism, using an object to stand for something else

Ⓑ   Hyperbole, using exaggeration to make a point

Ⓒ   Repetition, repeating words, phrases, or lines

Ⓓ   Flashback, referring back to an event in the past

32   Why does the poet compare the lily to a bride?

Ⓐ   To show how special the lily feels

Ⓑ   To emphasize how white the lily is

Ⓒ   To explain that the lily is being used in a wedding

Ⓓ   To suggest that the lily moves slowly

33   Read these lines from the poem.

> **Little White Lily**
> **Drooping with pain,**
> **Waiting and waiting**
> **For the wet rain.**

These lines suggest that the lily feels –

Ⓐ   confident

Ⓑ   desperate

Ⓒ   calm

Ⓓ   angry

34 In which stanza does the lily feel about the same as in the first stanza?

Ⓐ Stanza 3

Ⓑ Stanza 5

Ⓒ Stanza 8

Ⓓ Stanza 10

35 The poet probably uses the word <u>drooping</u> in the first stanza to create a sense of –

Ⓐ sadness

Ⓑ determination

Ⓒ loneliness

Ⓓ relaxation

Writing a Short Story
By Kevin Baker

Writing short stories is a popular and satisfying hobby for a lot of people. It is also an excellent way to express creative thoughts. Writing a good story is not easy, but it is certainly worth the effort. Here are the steps to take to write a good story.

Step 1

Every story starts with an idea. Start by thinking about the things that you enjoy. These activities are excellent subjects to base your stories on. Other ideas can come from thinking about subjects that you'd like to know more about.

Step 2

Once you have an idea, you can then decide who your main characters are going to be. Consider having both a hero and a villain in your story. This will help to keep your readers interested. A hero is also known as a protagonist, while a villain is known as an antagonist. You'll also need to think of the best location for your story to take place.

Step 3

Before you start writing, you need to plan your story. Most writers plan their stories by creating an outline. An outline is like an overview of the story. It should describe the main events that occur. Your story should have a beginning, a middle, and an end. This will help anyone who reads the story to follow its events.

Step 4

Now that you have your outline, it is time to start writing. Follow your outline and write your story. At this point, your story does not have to be perfect. You will go back and improve it later.

Step 5

The story you have written is your first draft. The next step is to read through it and revise it. Here are some questions to help you decide what might need to be changed:

- Are the events that happen clear?
- Is the story interesting?
- Have I described the characters well?
- Can I use better descriptions to make it more exciting?
- Have I left out any important points?
- Is the start of the story good enough to get the reader interested?
- Would the ending leave the reader feeling satisfied?

Keep working on your story until it is the best you can make it.

Step 6

Once the story is complete, read it in full to ensure that it is well-written and easy to follow. Make sure that all your sentences flow well and are easy to understand. You should also check for any spelling or grammar mistakes.

Step 7

It is now time to get some feedback on your story. Have others read your story so that they can make suggestions for improvements. Think about the advice that people tell you. You do not have to take all the advice given, but you should think about it.

Step 8

Revise your story again based on the feedback you have been given. You should also read through it again to make sure all your sentences are written correctly and to ensure that there are no spelling or grammar errors.

You should now have a well-written, polished, and entertaining story.

36 Read this sentence from the passage.

> **You should now have a well-written, polished, and entertaining story.**

What does the word <u>polished</u> show about the story?

Ⓐ   It is enjoyable to read.

Ⓑ   It has a suitable ending.

Ⓒ   It has been well-planned.

Ⓓ   It is smooth and free from errors.

37 Read this sentence from the passage.

> **It is also an excellent way to express creative thoughts.**

Which meaning of the word <u>express</u> is used in the sentence?

Ⓐ   To send something quickly

Ⓑ   To put into words

Ⓒ   Plain or clear

Ⓓ   Direct or fast

38 Which detail about the author would best suggest that the advice in the passage can be trusted?

Ⓐ   He has kept a diary of his thoughts for many years.

Ⓑ   He has a college degree.

Ⓒ   His favorite hobby is reading.

Ⓓ   He has successfully published many short stories.

39   What is the main purpose of the passage?

  Ⓐ   To teach readers how to do something

  Ⓑ   To encourage people to read more

  Ⓒ   To explain the purpose of writing

  Ⓓ   To compare different types of hobbies

40   Why does the author use bullet points in the passage?

  Ⓐ   To highlight the main points

  Ⓑ   To list a set of ideas

  Ⓒ   To show steps to follow in order

  Ⓓ   To describe items that are needed

41   In which step is the first draft of the story written?

  Ⓐ   Step 3

  Ⓑ   Step 4

  Ⓒ   Step 5

  Ⓓ   Step 6

42 According to the passage, what is a protagonist?

Ⓐ   The villain of a story

Ⓑ   The author of a story

Ⓒ   The hero of a story

Ⓓ   The reader of a story

43 According to the passage, what should you do first when writing a story?

Ⓐ   Decide who the main character is going to be

Ⓑ   Write an outline of the story

Ⓒ   Discuss your story idea with other people

Ⓓ   Think of an idea for the story

Directions: Read the next two passages. Then answer the questions.

A New Start

August 2, 2013

Dear Aunt Jamie,

What a day! I started at my new school this morning and had the best time. I made lots of new friends and really liked my teachers. I was so nervous the night before, but I had no reason to be. Everyone was so friendly and polite. They made me feel at ease. It was like I'd been at the school for a hundred years!

The day started very early at exactly 7 o'clock. I didn't want to feel rushed, so I made sure to get up early. I had my breakfast downstairs with my mom. She could tell that I was very anxious. Mom kept asking me what was wrong. I admitted that I was scared that people wouldn't like me or that everyone would just ignore me. She told me I had nothing to worry about and that everyone was going to love me. If they didn't love me, Mom said to send them her way for a good talking to. I couldn't stop laughing.

My mom dropped me off at the school gates about ten minutes before the bell. A little blond girl got dropped off at the same time and started waving at me. She ran over and told me her name was Abigail. She was very nice and we became close straight away. We spent all morning together and began to chat to another girl called Stacey. The three of us sat together in class all day and we even made our way home together! It went so quickly. Our teacher told us that tomorrow we would really start learning and developing new skills.

It is late now so I am going to sleep, but I cannot wait until tomorrow! I feel as though I am really going to enjoy my time at my new school. I only hope that my new friends feel the same way too.

Lots of love,

Casey

A New Arrival

Today was a very exciting day for me and my family. It was the day that my new baby brother came home from the hospital.

I remember when I first learned that I was going to have a new baby brother. "I have great news Emma," my mother said. "You are going to be a big sister." I just stared at my mother and I didn't even smile. I really wasn't sure what to think, but I had all these thoughts running through my head. I worried that he would drive me crazy by crying all the time. I worried that my parents might want him to have my room. I even worried that Mom would be too busy to come and watch me at my dance competitions.

All those things I worried about seem ridiculous now. I soon forgot about most of them anyway. By the time he was ready to arrive, I didn't have a single worry. I was far too excited about getting to meet him. I was looking forward to being his big sister and helping to look after him.

My baby brother was born yesterday morning at 9:51. My father came home in the afternoon and was overjoyed. He weighed 8 pounds and 1 ounce and my parents named him Bradley. My dad says that he is the most beautiful baby. I could barely sleep the night before. I was so excited about Bradley coming home. Eventually, I drifted off to sleep just as the morning sun began to rise.

I woke up as usual today at 9 o'clock. I went downstairs and enjoyed some toast for breakfast. I knew that my father was collecting my mother and Bradley at 11:30. I watched TV for a while before trying to read one of my favorite books. Whatever I tried to do, I just could not take my mind off my newborn brother. I couldn't help but try to imagine what he must look like. In my mind, he had bright blond hair and sparkling blue eyes. I wondered whether he would understand who I was when he first saw me. My daydreaming was interrupted by my dad's voice. "Let's go Emma," he called. It was finally time to leave.

I headed out to the car and we drove toward the hospital. I couldn't stop talking as we made our way through the winding roads. The short trip to the hospital seemed to take forever. We finally arrived at the hospital. We made our way through the reception and headed to the maternity ward. As we arrived at the doors, I could see my mother at the far end. She held a small bundle wrapped in a blue blanket in her arms.

Mom just smiled as I reached the end of her bed. She looked tired but extremely happy. I just stared for a few moments before Mom asked me if I wanted to meet my brother! I couldn't stop smiling and reached out in an instant. Mom held out her arms and passed Bradley to me.

I took him in my arms and cradled his tiny little baby body. As I looked down, he slowly opened his eyes and gazed up at me. They were the deepest blue that anyone could ever imagine. As I stroked his face he began to smile softly. Dad told me that he looks just like me when I was born. The thought that I was ever that beautiful made me smile. Then Bradley slowly closed his eyes and drifted off to sleep.

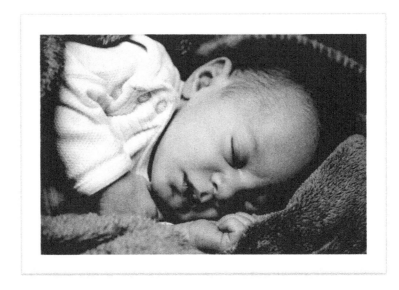

Directions: Use "A New Start" to answer the following questions.

44 Read this sentence from the letter.

She was very nice and we became close straight away.

What does Casey mean when she says that they "became close"?

Ⓐ   They began to be friends.

Ⓑ   They walked near each other.

Ⓒ   They stayed on their own.

Ⓓ   They were in the same class.

45 What will Casey most likely do when she arrives at school the next day?

Ⓐ   Sit by herself in the playground

Ⓑ   See if there are any other new people

Ⓒ   Look for Abigail and Stacey

Ⓓ   Go to class early to see her teacher

46 The reader can tell that Casey's mother —

Ⓐ   is used to meeting new people

Ⓑ   is very worried about her daughter

Ⓒ   cares about Casey's feelings

Ⓓ   wishes Casey did not have to start a new school

47   Which word would Casey most likely use to describe Abigail?

    Ⓐ   Funny

    Ⓑ   Friendly

    Ⓒ   Bossy

    Ⓓ   Shy

48   Casey writes that "It was like I'd been at the school for a hundred years!" What is the statement Casey makes used to show?

    Ⓐ   How bored Casey is

    Ⓑ   How comfortable Casey feels

    Ⓒ   How there is too much new information to take in

    Ⓓ   How the school has a long history

Directions: Use "A New Arrival" to answer the following questions.

49   Which word best describes the feelings created by the sentence below?

I took him in my arms and cradled his tiny little baby body.

Ⓐ   Loving

Ⓑ   Casual

Ⓒ   Lively

Ⓓ   Serious

50   Which word means about the same as <u>overjoyed</u>?

My father came home in the afternoon and was overjoyed.

Ⓐ   Tired

Ⓑ   Delighted

Ⓒ   Relaxed

Ⓓ   Gloomy

51   Why does Emma most likely say that the trip to the hospital "seemed to take forever"?

Ⓐ   Her father got lost on the way.

Ⓑ   She was nervous about seeing her brother.

Ⓒ   She was excited and impatient.

Ⓓ   She lived far from the hospital.

Directions: Use both "A New Start" and "A New Arrival" to answer the following questions.

52   Which word would both Casey and Emma use to describe their day?

   Ⓐ   Stressful

   Ⓑ   Positive

   Ⓒ   Thrilling

   Ⓓ   Bizarre

53   Which of these describes the main way the passages are similar?

   Ⓐ   They were both written to persuade people to appreciate family and friends.

   Ⓑ   They both describe how a main character solves a problem in her life.

   Ⓒ   They are both a first-person account of an important day in someone's life.

   Ⓓ   They both reveal how people grow and become stronger when facing challenges.

54   Both of the passages have a message about –

   Ⓐ   accepting change

   Ⓑ   showing kindness

   Ⓒ   taking things too seriously

   Ⓓ   sharing special moments

END OF SESSION 2

Section 4: Reading Practice Test 2

INTRODUCTION TO THE READING PRACTICE TEST
For Parents, Teachers, and Tutors

How Reading is Assessed by the State of Texas

The STAAR Reading test assesses reading skills by having students read literary and informational passages and answer questions about the passages. On the actual STAAR test, students will read 4 or 5 individual passages, as well as 1 or 2 sets of paired passages. Students will answer a total of 44 multiple-choice questions.

About the STAAR Reading Practice Test

This section of the book contains a practice test similar to the real STAAR Reading test. To ensure that all skills are tested, it is slightly longer than the real test. It has 5 individual passages, 1 set of paired passages, and a total of 54 questions. The questions cover all the skills tested on the STAAR Reading test, and have the same formats.

Taking the Test

Students are given 4 hours to complete the actual STAAR Reading test. Individual schools are allowed to determine their own schedule, though the test must be completed on the same school day. Schools may choose to include breaks or to complete the test in two or more sessions.

This practice test is designed to be taken in two sessions of 2 hours each. You can use the same time limit, or you can choose not to time the test. In real testing situations, students will complete the two sessions on the same day. You can follow this schedule, or you can choose your own schedule.

Students complete the STAAR Reading test by marking their answers on an answer sheet. An answer sheet is included in the back of the book.

Reading Skills

The STAAR Reading test assesses a specific set of skills. These skills are described in the TEKS, or Texas Essential Knowledge and Skills. The full answer key at the end of the book identifies the specific skill that each question is testing.

STAAR Reading

Practice Test 2

Session 1

Instructions

Read the passages. Each passage is followed by questions.

Read each question carefully. Then select the best answer. Fill in the circle for the best answer.

The River Bank Creative Writing Group

Creative writing is a great way of expressing yourself. The problem is that many people never try to write. Many people believe that they do not have the ability. At the River Bank Creative Writing Group, we aim to unleash your creativity.

We are based in Brooklyn, New York. We started our community organization in the fall of 2001. In the years since then, we have brought creative writing into the lives of many local residents. It does not matter whether you wish to write creatively as a hobby or as a way of making money. We have experienced and skilled staff to help you achieve success. We start by teaching the very basics of creative writing. Then we develop a program that is unique to your skills and goals. This can focus on writing short stories, poetry, plays, or anything else that interests you.

So what exactly do we offer? Well, our creative workshops are known for their quality. Our teachers include experienced professional writers and editors. They will guide you and help you get started. They will also offer feedback on your writing to help you improve. We also have guest speakers who attend once a week and share their own advice and experience. These are usually published authors who have achieved success in their fields. Our guest list is varied and includes successful poets, short story writers, and novelists. Their practical experience is the key to unlocking your creative talents.

We have achieved some great results at the River Bank Creative Writing Group. In 2005, one of our earliest students had her first novel published. She has since gone on to enjoy two further publications and is known worldwide. In 2009, another of our writers had his first poetry collection published. Thousands of our other writers have emerged from our classes as skilled creative writers.

Our classes can benefit you regardless of your goals. If you wish to unlock your creative skill for an exciting pastime, then we can help you. If you dream of being a published author, then we can help you make that happen. It has never been easier to unlock your creativity. If you have an interest in creative writing, then contact us today. We are waiting to hear from you and ready to help you on your journey!

1   In the sentence below, what does the word <u>unleash</u> mean?

> **At the River Bank Creative Writing Group, we aim to unleash your creativity.**

- Ⓐ   Take control of
- Ⓑ   Train and shape
- Ⓒ   Set free
- Ⓓ   Benefit from

2   What is the main purpose of the fourth paragraph?
- Ⓐ   To encourage people to take writing seriously
- Ⓑ   To show the success of the writing group
- Ⓒ   To describe different types of writing styles
- Ⓓ   To suggest that getting published is easy

3   What does the picture at the end of the passage most likely symbolize?
- Ⓐ   How long the writing group has existed for
- Ⓑ   How much of an achievement writing a book could be
- Ⓒ   How the teachers at the group are very experienced
- Ⓓ   How the writing group offers a range of services

4   From the information in the passage, the reader can conclude that the writing group –

Ⓐ   is mainly for young writers

Ⓑ   offers the services for free

Ⓒ   is suited to all types of writers

Ⓓ   considers publishing writers' works

5   The passage was probably written mainly to –

Ⓐ   encourage people to attend the writing group's classes

Ⓑ   highlight the benefits of creative writing

Ⓒ   describe the history of the creative writing group

Ⓓ   convince successful writers to be guest speakers

6   Read these sentences from the passage.

> **If you wish to unlock your creative skill for an exciting pastime, then we can help you. If you dream of being a published author, then we can help you make that happen.**

Why does the author most likely make these claims?

Ⓐ   To warn the reader that the workshops may be difficult

Ⓑ   To excite the reader about what may be possible

Ⓒ   To suggest that the reader should have a clear goal

Ⓓ   To describe the successes of past students

7   Which word best describes the tone of the passage?

Ⓐ   Comforting

Ⓑ   Straightforward

Ⓒ   Encouraging

Ⓓ   Modest

8   Which sentence best supports the idea that the River Bank Creative Writing Group tailors programs to suit each individual?

Ⓐ   *In the years since then, we have brought creative writing into the lives of many local residents.*

Ⓑ   *We have experienced and skilled staff to help you achieve success.*

Ⓒ   *We start by teaching the very basics of creative writing.*

Ⓓ   *Then we develop a program that is unique to your skills and goals.*

9   Which sentence from the passage is a fact?

Ⓐ   *Creative writing is a great way of expressing yourself.*

Ⓑ   *We started our community organization in the fall of 2001.*

Ⓒ   *Their practical experience is the key to unlocking your creative talents.*

Ⓓ   *It has never been easier to unlock your creativity.*

The Bees, the Wasps, and the Hornet

A store of honey had been found in a hollow tree. The wasps stated that it belonged to them. The bees were just as sure that the treasure was theirs. The argument grew very heated. It looked as if the affair could not be settled. But at last, with much good sense, they agreed to let a judge decide the matter. They brought the case before Judge Hornet.

When Judge Hornet called the case, witnesses stated that they had seen certain winged creatures in the neighborhood of the hollow tree. The creatures had hummed loudly, had striped bodies, and were yellow and black.

The wasps stated that this described them. The bees stated that this described them.

This did not help Judge Hornet make a decision. He said he wanted to take a few days to think about the case. When the case came up again, both sides had a large number of witnesses.

Judge Hornet sighed. He knew it was going to be a long day. Then the eldest bee asked if he could address the court.

"I'll allow it," Judge Hornet said.

"Your honor," the eldest bee said, "the case has now been going on for a week. If it is not decided soon, the honey will not be fit for anything. I move that the bees and the wasps be both instructed to make some honey. Then we shall soon see to whom the honey really belongs."

The wasps began to panic. They jumped up and down and complained loudly. Judge Hornet quickly understood why they did so.

"It is clear," said Judge Hornet, "who made the honey and who could not have made it. The honey belongs to the bees."

10 Read this sentence from the passage.

The argument grew very heated.

The word <u>heated</u> suggests that the bees and wasps became –

Ⓐ confused

Ⓑ angry

Ⓒ warm

Ⓓ tired

11 In the sentence below, why does the author use the word <u>treasure</u>?

The bees were just as sure that the treasure was theirs.

Ⓐ To suggest that the honey was gold

Ⓑ To show that the honey was hidden

Ⓒ To show that the honey had been there a long time

Ⓓ To suggest that the honey was precious

12 What is the main purpose of the first paragraph?

Ⓐ To describe the main problem

Ⓑ To compare the bees and the wasps

Ⓒ To introduce the setting

Ⓓ To describe how to solve an argument

13   The main lesson the wasps learn is about being –

Ⓐ   hardworking

Ⓑ   honest

Ⓒ   prepared

Ⓓ   skilled

14   Which sentence shows that the passage has a third-person omniscient point of view?

Ⓐ   *A store of honey had been found in a hollow tree.*

Ⓑ   *They brought the case before Judge Hornet.*

Ⓒ   *The bees stated that this described them.*

Ⓓ   *Judge Hornet quickly understood why they did so.*

15   How is the passage mainly organized?

Ⓐ   Two events are compared and contrasted.

Ⓑ   Events are described in the order they occur.

Ⓒ   Facts are given to support an argument.

Ⓓ   A question is asked and then answered.

16   Why do the wasps most likely panic when the elder bee suggests that the judge should instruct the bees and wasps to make honey?

Ⓐ   The wasps know they cannot make honey.

Ⓑ   The wasps are too tired to make honey.

Ⓒ   The wasps think the bees' honey will taste better.

Ⓓ   The wasps think it will take too long.

17   Based on his suggestion that the bees and the wasps both be instructed to make honey, the eldest bee is best described as –

Ⓐ   impatient

Ⓑ   polite

Ⓒ   wise

Ⓓ   cranky

18   The passage states that "when the case came up again, both sides had a large number of witnesses." How does this influence the events?

Ⓐ   It makes the wasps sorry for their actions because they realize how much the bees care about the honey.

Ⓑ   It makes the wasps upset and nervous because they fear being embarrassed in front of so many people.

Ⓒ   It makes the judge want to be sure to make the right decision because he knows how important it must be to both sides.

Ⓓ   It makes the judge open to listening to the ideas of the eldest bee because the judge wants to find a faster solution.

Take a Deep Breath

The lung is an organ that is used to help many living things breathe. Humans have two lungs in their body. The lungs have several important purposes. The main purpose of the lungs is to take in oxygen from the air. Carbon dioxide leaves the body via the lungs. The lungs are also used to protect the heart from any sudden shocks to the chest. Another purpose of the lungs is to filter blood clots.

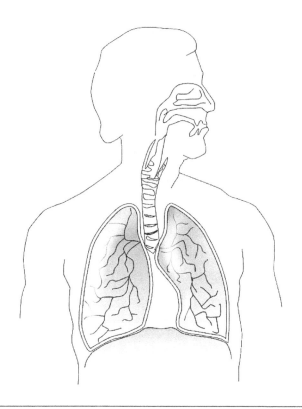

Looking After the Lungs

It is important to take good care of your lungs. One of the best ways to keep your lungs healthy is to exercise often. This gives your lungs a workout! The more you exercise, the stronger your lungs will become!

The lungs are so important that your body has built-in ways of protecting them. Have you ever breathed in dust? What happened? Have you heard of people who are affected by pollen in the air? If there is anything getting into the body from the air, your body has special ways of dealing with it. One way is to cough, which removes particles from the lungs and breathing passages. The other way is to sneeze, which removes particles from the nasal cavity and nose.

Sneezing is a bodily reflex similar to a cough. It serves the same purpose of a cough, which is to remove foreign bodies and irritants from the body. However, a sneeze is much more powerful than a cough. In fact, the air leaving the body from a sneeze can travel at speeds of up to 100 miles per hour!

A sneeze occurs when air is rapidly expelled, or removed from, the lungs. The scientific term for sneezing is sternutation. There are four main reasons that people sneeze.

- Irritation – people sneeze when something irritates the nose. This is the body's way of cleaning the nose and stopping irritants from getting into the lungs.
- Light – people can sneeze when they are suddenly exposed to bright light.
- Feeling full – some people have a very rare condition where they sneeze as a response to feeling very full after a meal.
- Infection – many infections by viruses, including the common cold, can cause people to sneeze. The purpose of the sneeze is to remove virus particles from the body.

The most common reason people sneeze is due to irritation. Many people sneeze when they breathe in dust, pollen, or other irritants. This condition is known as hay fever, and is most common in spring when there is a lot of pollen in the air.

For some people, spring flowers are a wonderful sign that the cold weather of winter and fall has passed. For others, flowers means the beginning of hay fever season.

19   Which sentence states the main idea of the first paragraph?

    Ⓐ   *Humans have two lungs in their body.*

    Ⓑ   *The lungs have several important purposes.*

    Ⓒ   *Carbon dioxide leaves the body via the lungs.*

    Ⓓ   *Another purpose of the lungs is to filter blood clots.*

20   What is the main purpose of the information in the box?

    Ⓐ   To give advice on how to have healthy lungs

    Ⓑ   To describe one of the purposes of the lungs

    Ⓒ   To describe the two human lungs

    Ⓓ   To show that lungs are important organs

21   Which of the following should NOT be added to the web to summarize the information in the passage?

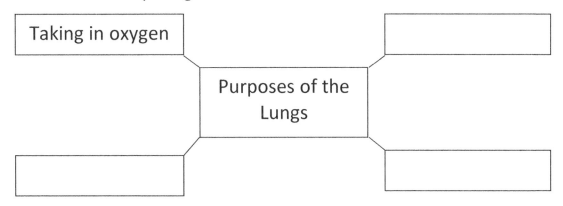

    Ⓐ   Removing carbon dioxide

    Ⓑ   Making energy

    Ⓒ   Protecting the heart

    Ⓓ   Filtering blood clots

22   How is the paragraph below mainly organized?

> **Sneezing is a bodily reflex similar to a cough. It serves the same purpose of a cough, which is to remove foreign bodies and irritants from the body. However, a sneeze is much more powerful than a cough. In fact, the air leaving the body from a sneeze can travel at speeds of up to 100 miles per hour!**

Ⓐ   A problem is described and then a solution is given.

Ⓑ   Events are described in the order they occur.

Ⓒ   Facts are given to support an argument.

Ⓓ   Two events are compared.

23   The photograph at the end of the passage mainly relates to which cause of sneezing?

Ⓐ   Irritation

Ⓑ   Light

Ⓒ   Feeling full

Ⓓ   Infection

24   Which term best describes the sentence below?

> **The scientific term for sneezing is sternutation.**

Ⓐ   Comparison

Ⓑ   Definition

Ⓒ   Exaggeration

Ⓓ   Assumption

25 How does the diagram help show how sneezing would clean the nose?

Ⓐ It shows how the lungs can hold a lot of air.

Ⓑ It shows how air only moves in one direction.

Ⓒ It shows how quickly the air would be traveling.

Ⓓ It shows how air from the lungs would travel through the nose.

26 According to the passage, which reason for sneezing is least common?

Ⓐ Irritation

Ⓑ Light

Ⓒ Feeling full

Ⓓ Infection

27 Read this dictionary entry for the word <u>foreign</u>.

> **foreign** *adjective*
> 1. located outside of one's own country 2. concerned with another country or area 3. unfamiliar or not known to a person 4. located in an abnormal place

Which definition of the word <u>foreign</u> is used in the sentence below?

> **It serves the same purpose of a cough, which is to remove foreign bodies and irritants from the body.**

Ⓐ Definition 1

Ⓑ Definition 2

Ⓒ Definition 3

Ⓓ Definition 4

END OF SESSION 1

STAAR Reading

Practice Test 2

Session 2

Instructions
Read the passages. Each passage is followed by questions.
Read each question carefully. Then select the best answer. Fill in the circle for the best answer.

Trying Too Hard

Robert was determined to do well in his exams. He devoted all of his spare time to study. He had always wanted to be a lawyer when he grew up. He wanted to go to a good college and enjoy a successful career. Unfortunately, this meant that he was almost always serious. Even though he was young, he was unable to relax and enjoy himself most of the time. His friends often got frustrated that he didn't want to spend much time with them.

Robert had an important exam the following day. He had spent almost an entire week preparing for it. He had managed to get little sleep and was very tired.

He even spent the night before the exam revising and had barely managed any sleep at all. However, he thought that he was ready for the exam. He was confident that he had worked harder than anyone else and was sure to get a perfect grade.

After Robert ate his breakfast, he started to feel a little ill. He was tired and unable to focus. He also had a small headache and found it very difficult to concentrate. He still refused to believe that he could ever fail the exam. Robert arrived at the school hall and took his seat beside his friends. He noticed how relaxed and happy they looked compared to him.

"They are just underprepared," he thought to himself as he began the exam.

Despite his best efforts, Robert struggled. The numbers seemed to swim in front of him. After twenty minutes, he felt very hot and uncomfortable. He then slumped in his chair, and one of his friends called for help. The school doctor suggested that he was exhausted and would be unable to complete the exam.

He spent the lunch break in the nurse's office. He looked out the window and watched his friends. They smiled and joked and seemed to have not a care in the world. Robert decided that from then on, he wouldn't take it quite so seriously. He would study enough, but never too much.

28   What does the word <u>frustrated</u> mean in the sentence below?

His friends often got frustrated that he didn't want to spend much time with them.

Ⓐ   Worried

Ⓑ   Annoyed

Ⓒ   Confused

Ⓓ   Amused

29   What does the word <u>underprepared</u> mean in the sentence below?

"They are just underprepared," he thought to himself as he began the exam.

Ⓐ   The most prepared

Ⓑ   More prepared

Ⓒ   Not prepared enough

Ⓓ   Too prepared

30   Think about the genre of "Trying Too Hard." What is the main feature the passage shares with a fable?

Ⓐ   It features mythical creatures.

Ⓑ   It involves forces of nature.

Ⓒ   It has a moral lesson.

Ⓓ   It is set in the past.

31   Which sentence best explains why Robert feels ill during the exam?

Ⓐ   *Robert had an important exam the following day.*

Ⓑ   *He had spent almost an entire week preparing for it.*

Ⓒ   *He even spent the night before the exam revising and had barely managed any sleep at all.*

Ⓓ   *He was confident that he had worked harder than anyone else and was sure to get a perfect grade.*

32   What happens right after Robert slumps in his chair?

Ⓐ   He keeps working on the exam.

Ⓑ   The nurse comes to see him.

Ⓒ   He starts to feel sick.

Ⓓ   His friend calls for help.

33   Which of these describes the main lesson that Robert learns in the passage?

Ⓐ   It is important to have a balanced life.

Ⓑ   It is better to have fun than to do well.

Ⓒ   You should never give up on your goals.

Ⓓ   You can achieve anything if you believe in yourself.

34   Which sentence from the passage best summarizes the lesson you selected in Question 33?

Ⓐ   *Robert was determined to do well in his exams.*

Ⓑ   *He still refused to believe that he could ever fail the exam.*

Ⓒ   *They smiled and joked and seemed to have not a care in the world.*

Ⓓ   *He would study enough, but never too much.*

35   Which statement correctly completes the diagram below?

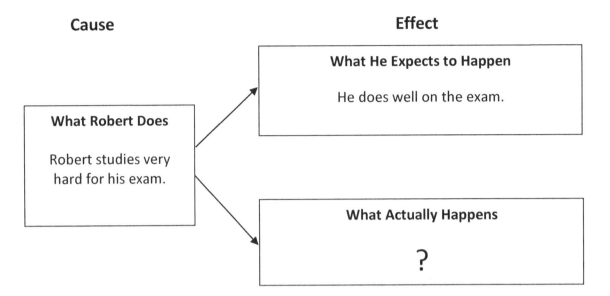

Ⓐ   He fails the exam.

Ⓑ   He gets a perfect score.

Ⓒ   He does not complete the exam.

Ⓓ   He decides he doesn't care about the exam.

36   How would the ending of the passage most likely be different if it was told from Robert's point of view?

Ⓐ   The reader would have a better understanding of Robert's feelings about what happened.

Ⓑ   The reader would realize that Robert is probably not really going to change.

Ⓒ   The reader would worry more about whether or not Robert will be allowed to retake the exam.

Ⓓ   The reader would not feel sorry for Robert since what happened was his own fault.

A Pen Pal Replies

Dear Mary,

I hope that you are well. It was so nice to read your letter the other day. I have always dreamed about having a pen pal. It is even better that you live in such a peaceful place and have such a different life to mine. Hopefully, we can learn from each other and grow to be the very best of friends. Life in New York is so busy and it is difficult to find the time to really get to know people. Even becoming close to my classmates has proved to be quite difficult over the years. It is my wish that our letters will let us get to know each other and share parts of our lives.

Your horse Shannon sounds beautiful. I adore animals and am very jealous that you get to live on a farm. I cannot imagine how much fun it is to ride a horse through endless fields and meadows. I would love to come and visit you one day. This must seem strange to you, but I would have to travel miles just to see some farmland. Your siblings also sound lovely. I am an only child, so I can only imagine what it is like to have older brothers and sisters. I bet they look after you and keep you safe. I am sorry to hear that your older brother is leaving for university in England though. At least he will be able to visit you on the weekends. He will probably bring back lots of presents for you and your family!

You would find New York fascinating. I live in a two-bedroom apartment on the tenth floor of our building. New York is very busy, but at times it can be the most amazing city in the whole wide world. At night it is so bright and lively and the whole place is full of things to do. I think I will be able to appreciate it even more when I am older.

My parents say that we may be going to Florida in the fall. I have been there before and it is the perfect place to take a vacation. There are so many children who are our age and it is easy to make new and interesting friends.

I love reading too! I have never read any books by your favorite author Enid Blyton though. I will have to go to my local library and find some. I love mystery books and science fiction novels too. I also enjoy dancing and often enter competitions. I even managed to win a first place trophy last year. My other favorite hobby is ice skating. In winter, I skate in Central Park. In the other seasons, I go to an indoor rink. I am hoping to start entering ice skating competitions next year.

Anyway, I have to go now and do my homework. I have enclosed a photograph of myself and my home address so you can write to me again. I really hope that I hear from you soon!

Lots of love,

Megan

37   As it is used below, which word means the opposite of <u>adore</u>?

I adore animals and am very jealous that you get to live on a farm.

Ⓐ   Fear

Ⓑ   Love

Ⓒ   Hate

Ⓓ   Admire

38   Which words in the sentence show that Megan is exaggerating?

I cannot imagine how much fun it is to ride a horse through endless fields and meadows.

Ⓐ   "cannot imagine"

Ⓑ   "how much fun"

Ⓒ   "ride a horse"

Ⓓ   "endless fields and meadows"

39   How is Mary similar to Megan?

Ⓐ   She lives in the country.

Ⓑ   She likes reading.

Ⓒ   She dances.

Ⓓ   She has an older brother.

40   According to the letter, where is Mary's brother going to university?

Ⓐ   France

Ⓑ   Florida

Ⓒ   England

Ⓓ   Italy

41   Which of the following completes the web below?

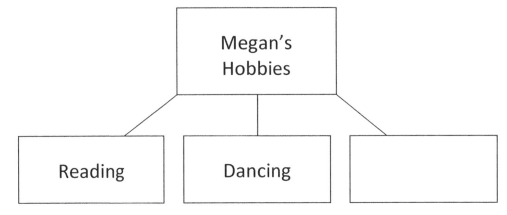

Ⓐ   Horse riding

Ⓑ   Ice skating

Ⓒ   Singing

Ⓓ   Cooking

42   Which conclusion can be made based on the letter?

Ⓐ   Mary and Megan have just become pen pals.

Ⓑ   Megan has pen pals all over the world.

Ⓒ   Mary plans to visit Megan in New York.

Ⓓ   Megan has been writing to Mary for years.

43   In which sentence does Megan only give factual information?

Ⓐ   *You would find New York fascinating.*

Ⓑ   *I live in a two-bedroom apartment on the tenth floor of our building.*

Ⓒ   *New York is very busy, but at times it can be the most amazing city in the whole wide world.*

Ⓓ   *At night it is so bright and lively and the whole place is full of things to do.*

Directions: Read the next two passages. Then answer the questions.

The Super Bowl

The Super Bowl is the deciding game of the National Football League (NFL). It decides who wins the championship trophy each season. It was first played in the winter of 1967 to find the champion of the 1966 season. Since that time, it has become a major national occasion loved by football fans everywhere. It is a major honor to win the Super Bowl for both teams and their supporters.

At the time it was created, there were two American football leagues. These were the NFL and the AFL, or American Football League. The winners of each league would play against each other to determine which team was the overall champion.

When the two leagues merged, the game was retained. It has since become a game where the top national teams play each other for the main championship. The Green Bay Packers won the first two Super Bowls played in 1967 and 1968. They were considered to be the best team at the time. Many people thought they would continue to win for years to come. This changed in 1969 when the New York Jets won Super Bowl III. This was the last Super Bowl that included teams from separate NFL and AFL leagues.

The game has grown steadily in popularity since this time. It is played annually on a Sunday. The timing of the game has changed since 1970. While it used to be played in early January, it is now played on the first Sunday in February. The Super Bowl game has become a major part of America's culture. It has even been declared a national holiday across the nation.

The Super Bowl has emerged as the most watched television event in America. Super Bowl XLV was played in 2011 and drew a national audience of more than 110 million viewers. The Super Bowl is also one of the most watched sporting events throughout the world. Only the UEFA Champions League trophy in soccer is viewed by a higher global audience.

The Pittsburgh Steelers have won a total of six Super Bowls. They stand alone as the most successful team in the contest's history. The Dallas Cowboys and the San Francisco 49ers have each won the trophy five times. The Pittsburgh Steelers had a chance to win a seventh title in the 2011 Super Bowl. However, they were defeated by the Green Bay Packers. It was the fourth win for the Green Bay Packers.

Sports and Trophies

Trophies are an important part of major sporting leagues. They become a symbol of what every team hopes to achieve and act as a lasting symbol of the winning team's achievements. They often have a long history that makes them even more special.

The Vince Lombardi Trophy

The team that wins the Super Bowl receives the Vince Lombardi Trophy. It is named after the coach of the Green Bay Packers who won the first two Super Bowl games. It was designed by the vice president of Tiffany & Co. in 1966 and the trophies have been made by the company ever since.

It was first presented to the Green Bay Packers in 1967, though it was simply known as the championship trophy at that time. Its name was changed in 1970 after Vince Lombardi passed away. Unlike some other trophies, a new Vince Lombardi trophy is made each year and the winning team keeps that trophy forever.

The Larry O'Brien Championship Trophy

The Larry O'Brien Championship Trophy is awarded to the winning team of the National Basketball Association (NBA) finals each year. The name of the winning team and the year is engraved on the trophy, and given to the winning team to keep. The trophy is named after Larry O'Brien, who was the NBA commissioner from 1975 to 1984.

The trophy is made by Tiffany & Co. each year. It is made from silver alloys and coated in 24 karat gold. The golden color of the trophy is striking and distinguishes it from other trophies. However, despite its striking appearance, it is not as well known as many other sporting trophies.

The Stanley Cup

The Stanley Cup is the most appreciated ice hockey trophy in the world. It is awarded every year to the winner of the National Hockey League (NHL) championships.

Unlike most other sports, a new Stanley Cup is not made each year. Instead, the winning team keeps the trophy until new champions are crowned the next year. This ability to take possession of the trophy for a short time makes players appreciate the award even more. Each winning team also has the names of players, coaches, and other team staff engraved on the trophy. This is considered a great honor by all.

The Stanley Cup is the oldest professional sports trophy in North America. It was donated by the Governor General of Canada, Lord Stanley of Preston, in 1892.

Directions: Use "The Super Bowl" to answer the following questions.

44 According to the passage, how has the Super Bowl changed since it was introduced?

Ⓐ   It is watched by less people.

Ⓑ   It is played between more teams.

Ⓒ   It is played in a different month.

Ⓓ   It is held on a Saturday.

45 How is the third paragraph mainly organized?

Ⓐ   A problem is described and then a solution is given.

Ⓑ   Events are described in the order they occurred.

Ⓒ   Two teams are compared and contrasted.

Ⓓ   Facts are given to support an argument.

46 According to the passage, which team has won the most Super Bowls?

Ⓐ   Green Bay Packers

Ⓑ   Pittsburgh Steelers

Ⓒ   Dallas Cowboys

Ⓓ   New York Jets

47   Which meaning of the word <u>drew</u> is used in the sentence below?

> **Super Bowl XLV was played in 2011 and drew a national audience of more than 110 million viewers.**

  Ⓐ   Attracted

  Ⓑ   Sketched

  Ⓒ   Dragged

  Ⓓ   Tied

48   Which statement made in paragraph 1 is best supported by the paragraph below?

> **The Super Bowl has emerged as the most watched television event in America. Super Bowl XLV was played in 2011 and drew a national audience of more than 110 million viewers. The Super Bowl is also one of the most watched sporting events throughout the world. Only the UEFA Champions League trophy in soccer is viewed by a higher global audience.**

  Ⓐ   *The Super Bowl is the deciding game of the National Football League (NFL).*

  Ⓑ   *It was first played in the winter of 1967 to find the champion of the 1966 season.*

  Ⓒ   *Since that time, it has become a major national occasion loved by football fans everywhere.*

  Ⓓ   *It is a major honor to win the Super Bowl for both teams and their supporters.*

Directions: Use "Sports and Trophies" to answer the following questions.

49   In the sentence below, which word could best be used in place of <u>appreciate</u>?

> **This ability to take possession of the trophy for a short time makes players appreciate the award even more.**

    Ⓐ   Notice

    Ⓑ   Demand

    Ⓒ   Ignore

    Ⓓ   Value

50   How does the last paragraph of "The Stanley Cup" help show the importance of the trophy?

    Ⓐ   It shows that ice hockey has been played for a long time.

    Ⓑ   It shows that ice hockey is a national sport.

    Ⓒ   It shows the long history of the trophy.

    Ⓓ   It shows that the trophy is most important to Canadians.

51   Which sentence from the passage is an opinion?

    Ⓐ   *It is awarded every year to the winner of the National Hockey League (NHL) championships.*

    Ⓑ   *This ability to take possession of the trophy makes players appreciate the award even more.*

    Ⓒ   *The Stanley Cup is the oldest professional sports trophy in North America.*

    Ⓓ   *It was donated by the Governor General of Canada, Lord Stanley of Preston, in 1892.*

Directions: Use both "The Super Bowl" and "Sports and Trophies" to answer the following questions.

52 Which inference can best be made based on the information in both passages?

    Ⓐ Vince Lombardi was a successful and respected coach.

    Ⓑ Vince Lombardi was replaced after the Green Bay Packers were defeated in 1969.

    Ⓒ Vince Lombardi still coaches the Green Bay Packers today.

    Ⓓ Vince Lombardi was a football player before he became a coach.

53 Both passages suggest the importance of which of the following in sports?

    Ⓐ Guidance and leadership

    Ⓑ History and tradition

    Ⓒ Hard work and determination

    Ⓓ Teamwork and trust

54 Which of these is a difference between the passages "The Super Bowl" and "Sports and Trophies"?

    Ⓐ "The Super Bowl" covers the history of an event, while "Sports and Trophies" only focuses on the present.

    Ⓑ "The Super Bowl" focuses on one popular sport, while "Sports and Trophies" covers several popular sports.

    Ⓒ "The Super Bowl" tries to persuade readers, while "Sports and Trophies" tries to inform readers.

    Ⓓ "The Super Bowl" describes positive features of sports, while "Sports and Trophies" describes negative features.

END OF SESSION 2

ANSWER KEY

The STAAR Reading test assesses a specific set of skills. These are described in the Texas Essential Knowledge and Skills, or TEKS. The TEKS are the state standards that describe what students should know and what students should be able to do.

The questions in this book cover all the TEKS standards that are assessed on the state test. The answer key that follows includes the TEKS standard that each question is testing. Use the skill listed with each question to identify areas of strength and weakness. Then target revision and instruction accordingly.

Section 1: Reading Mini-Tests

Mini-Test 1, Informational Text

Question	Answer	TEKS Standard
1	D	Use context to determine or clarify the meaning of unfamiliar or multiple meaning words.
2	B	Interpret details from procedural text to complete a task, solve a problem, or perform procedures.
3	A	Use multiple text features and graphics to gain an overview of the contents of text and to locate information.
4	A	Determine the meaning of grade-level academic English words derived from Latin, Greek, or other linguistic roots and affixes.
5	A	Summarize and paraphrase texts in ways that maintain meaning and logical order within a text and across texts.
6	D	Identify the author's viewpoint or position and explain the basic relationships among ideas in the argument.
7	C	Make inferences about text and use textual evidence to support understanding.
8	D	Interpret details from procedural text to complete a task, solve a problem, or perform procedures.
9	B	Analyze how the organizational pattern of a text influences the relationships among the ideas.
10	C	Synthesize and make logical connections between ideas within a text and across two or three texts representing similar or different genres.

Mini-Test 2, Literary Text

Question	Answer	TEKS Standard
1	A	Use context to determine or clarify the meaning of unfamiliar or multiple meaning words.
2	C	Explain different forms of third-person points of view in stories.
3	B	Make inferences about text and use textual evidence to support understanding.
4	C	Summarize and paraphrase texts in ways that maintain meaning and logical order within a text and across texts.
5	A	Analyze how poets use sound effects (e.g., alliteration, internal rhyme, onomatopoeia, rhyme scheme) to reinforce meaning in poems.
6	C	Analyze how poets use sound effects (e.g., alliteration, internal rhyme, onomatopoeia, rhyme scheme) to reinforce meaning in poems.
7	D	Make inferences about text and use textual evidence to support understanding.
8	B	Use context to determine or clarify the meaning of unfamiliar or multiple meaning words.
9	A	Evaluate the impact of sensory details, imagery, and figurative language in literary text.
10	B	Evaluate the impact of sensory details, imagery, and figurative language in literary text.

Mini-Test 3, Informational Text

Question	Answer	TEKS Standard
1	A	Use context to determine or clarify the meaning of unfamiliar or multiple meaning words.
2	D	Determine the facts in text and verify them through established methods.
3	C	Identify the author's viewpoint or position and explain the basic relationships among ideas in the argument.
4	D	Summarize the main ideas and supporting details in a text in ways that maintain meaning and logical order.
5	D	Recognize exaggerated, contradictory, or misleading statements in text.
6	C	Make inferences about text and use textual evidence to support understanding.
7	B	Synthesize and make logical connections between ideas within a text and across two or three texts representing similar or different genres.
8	D	Draw conclusions from the information presented by an author and evaluate how well the author's purpose was achieved.
9	B	Summarize and paraphrase texts in ways that maintain meaning and logical order within a text and across texts.
10	C	Analyze how the organizational pattern of a text influences the relationships among the ideas.

Mini-Test 4, Literary Text

Question	Answer	TEKS Standard
1	C	Use context to determine or clarify the meaning of unfamiliar or multiple meaning words.
2	C	Understand, make inferences and draw conclusions about the structure and elements of drama and provide evidence from text to support their understanding.
3	B	Evaluate the impact of sensory details, imagery, and figurative language in literary text.
4	B	Explain the roles and functions of characters in various plots, including their relationships and conflicts.
5	A	Evaluate the impact of sensory details, imagery, and figurative language in literary text.
6	B	Describe incidents that advance the story or novel, explaining how each incident gives rise to or foreshadows future events.
7	D	Explain different forms of third-person points of view in stories.
8	A	Explain the roles and functions of characters in various plots, including their relationships and conflicts.
9	B	Evaluate the impact of sensory details, imagery, and figurative language in literary text.
10	C	Explain the effect of a historical event or movement on the theme of a work of literature.

Mini-Test 5, Paired Literary Texts

Question	Answer	TEKS Standard
1	B	Use context to determine or clarify the meaning of unfamiliar or multiple meaning words.
2	A	Use context to determine or clarify the meaning of unfamiliar or multiple meaning words.
3	A	Understand, make inferences and draw conclusions about the structure and elements of drama and provide evidence from text to support their understanding.
4	B	Use context to determine or clarify the meaning of unfamiliar or multiple meaning words.
5	B	Evaluate the impact of sensory details, imagery, and figurative language in literary text.
6	C	Explain the roles and functions of characters in various plots, including their relationships and conflicts.
7	D	Describe incidents that advance the story or novel, explaining how each incident gives rise to or foreshadows future events.
8	D	Understand, make inferences and draw conclusions about the structure and elements of drama and provide evidence from text to support their understanding.
9	D	Explain different forms of third-person points of view in stories.
10	B	Compare and contrast the themes or moral lessons of several works of fiction from various cultures.
11	B	Make connections (e.g., thematic links, author analysis) between and across multiple texts of various genres and provide textual evidence.
12	B	Make connections (e.g., thematic links, author analysis) between and across multiple texts of various genres and provide textual evidence.

Mini-Test 6, Paired Informational Texts

Question	Answer	TEKS Standard
1	D	Use context to determine or clarify the meaning of unfamiliar or multiple meaning words.
2	D	Summarize the main ideas and supporting details in a text in ways that maintain meaning and logical order.
3	B	Use multiple text features and graphics to gain an overview of the contents of text and to locate information.
4	A	Analyze how the organizational pattern of a text influences the relationships among the ideas.
5	A	Determine the meaning of grade-level academic English words derived from Latin, Greek, or other linguistic roots and affixes.
6	B	Use context to determine or clarify the meaning of unfamiliar or multiple meaning words.
7	D	Interpret details from procedural text to complete a task, solve a problem, or perform procedures.
8	B	Draw conclusions from the information presented by an author and evaluate how well the author's purpose was achieved.
9	C	Make inferences about text and use textual evidence to support understanding.
10	A	Synthesize and make logical connections between ideas within a text and across two or three texts representing similar or different genres.
11	C	Make connections (e.g., thematic links, author analysis) between and across multiple texts of various genres and provide textual evidence.
12	A	Make connections (e.g., thematic links, author analysis) between and across multiple texts of various genres and provide textual evidence.

Section 2: Vocabulary Quizzes

Quiz 1: Use Context to Determine Word Meaning

Question	Answer	TEKS Standard
1	B	Use context (e.g., in-sentence restatement) to determine or clarify the meaning of unfamiliar or multiple meaning words.
2	A	
3	D	
4	D	
5	C	
6	B	
7	B	
8	C	
9	D	

Quiz 2: Understand and Use Multiple Meaning Words

Question	Answer	TEKS Standard
1	C	Use context (e.g., in-sentence restatement) to determine or clarify the meaning of unfamiliar or multiple meaning words.
2	D	
3	C	
4	B	
5	D	
6	B	

Quiz 3: Understand and Use Prefixes

Question	Answer	TEKS Standard
1	C	Determine the meaning of grade-level academic English words derived from Latin, Greek, or other linguistic roots and affixes.
2	C	
3	B	
4	B	
5	A	
6	B	
7	B	
8	D	

Quiz 4: Understand and Use Suffixes

Question	Answer	TEKS Standard
1	C	Determine the meaning of grade-level academic English words derived from Latin, Greek, or other linguistic roots and affixes.
2	A	
3	C	
4	D	
5	A	
6	A	
7	C	
8	C	

Quiz 5: Use Greek and Latin Roots

Question	Answer	TEKS Standard
1	A	Determine the meaning of grade-level academic English words derived from Latin, Greek, or other linguistic roots and affixes.
2	C	
3	C	
4	C	
5	D	
6	A	
7	C	

Quiz 6: Use a Dictionary, Glossary, or Thesaurus

Question	Answer	TEKS Standard
1	A	Use a dictionary, a glossary, or a thesaurus to determine the meanings, syllabication, pronunciations, alternate word choices, and parts of speech of words.
2	B	
3	C	
4	A	
5	B	

Section 3: STAAR Reading Practice Test 1

Practice Test 1, Session 1

Question	Answer	TEKS Standard
1	C	Use context to determine or clarify the meaning of unfamiliar or multiple meaning words.
2	A	Determine the meaning of grade-level academic English words derived from Latin, Greek, or other linguistic roots and affixes.
3	A	Analyze how the organizational pattern of a text influences the relationships among the ideas.
4	D	Use multiple text features and graphics to gain an overview of the contents of text and to locate information.
5	B	Summarize the main ideas and supporting details in a text in ways that maintain meaning and logical order.
6	B	Make inferences about text and use textual evidence to support understanding.
7	A	Draw conclusions from the information presented by an author and evaluate how well the author's purpose was achieved.
8	C	Summarize and paraphrase texts in ways that maintain meaning and logical order within a text and across texts.
9	A	Synthesize and make logical connections between ideas within a text and across two or three texts representing similar or different genres.
10	B	Use context to determine or clarify the meaning of unfamiliar or multiple meaning words.
11	D	Determine the meaning of grade-level academic English words derived from Latin, Greek, or other linguistic roots and affixes.
12	B	Make inferences about text and use textual evidence to support understanding.
13	B	Describe incidents that advance the story or novel, explaining how each incident gives rise to or foreshadows future events.
14	B	Evaluate the impact of sensory details, imagery, and figurative language in literary text.
15	B	Understand, make inferences and draw conclusions about the structure and elements of drama and provide evidence from text to support their understanding.
16	A	Explain the roles and functions of characters in various plots, including their relationships and conflicts.
17	C	Explain the roles and functions of characters in various plots, including their relationships and conflicts.
18	C	Summarize and paraphrase texts in ways that maintain meaning and logical order within a text and across texts.
19	A	Use context to determine or clarify the meaning of unfamiliar or multiple meaning words.
20	A	Use multiple text features and graphics to gain an overview of the contents of text and to locate information.

Question	Answer	TEKS Standard
21	B	Analyze how the organizational pattern of a text influences the relationships among the ideas.
22	A	Interpret factual or quantitative information presented in maps, charts, illustrations, graphs, timelines, tables, and diagrams.
23	D	Determine the facts in text and verify them through established methods.
24	B	Synthesize and make logical connections between ideas within a text and across two or three texts representing similar or different genres.
25	A	Interpret factual or quantitative information presented in maps, charts, illustrations, graphs, timelines, tables, and diagrams.
26	B	Identify the author's viewpoint or position and explain the basic relationships among ideas in the argument.
27	A	Use a dictionary, a glossary, or a thesaurus to determine the meanings, syllabication, pronunciations, alternate word choices, and parts of speech of words.

Practice Test 1, Session 2

Question	Answer	TEKS Standard
28	A	Explain the roles and functions of characters in various plots, including their relationships and conflicts.
29	A	Analyze how poets use sound effects (e.g., alliteration, internal rhyme, onomatopoeia, rhyme scheme) to reinforce meaning in poems.
30	D	Analyze how poets use sound effects (e.g., alliteration, internal rhyme, onomatopoeia, rhyme scheme) to reinforce meaning in poems.
31	C	Analyze how poets use sound effects (e.g., alliteration, internal rhyme, onomatopoeia, rhyme scheme) to reinforce meaning in poems.
32	B	Evaluate the impact of sensory details, imagery, and figurative language in literary text.
33	B	Evaluate the impact of sensory details, imagery, and figurative language in literary text.
34	B	Understand, make inferences and draw conclusions about the structure and elements of drama and provide evidence from text to support their understanding.
35	A	Use context to determine or clarify the meaning of unfamiliar or multiple meaning words.
36	D	Use context to determine or clarify the meaning of unfamiliar or multiple meaning words.
37	B	Use context to determine or clarify the meaning of unfamiliar or multiple meaning words.
38	D	Draw conclusions from the information presented by an author and evaluate how well the author's purpose was achieved.
39	A	Identify the author's viewpoint or position and explain the basic relationships among ideas in the argument.
40	B	Analyze how the organizational pattern of a text influences the relationships among the ideas.
41	B	Interpret details from procedural text to complete a task, solve a problem, or perform procedures.
42	A	Use multiple text features and graphics to gain an overview of the contents of text and to locate information.
43	D	Interpret details from procedural text to complete a task, solve a problem, or perform procedures.
44	A	Use context to determine or clarify the meaning of unfamiliar or multiple meaning words.
45	C	Make inferences about text and use textual evidence to support understanding.
46	C	Make inferences about text and use textual evidence to support understanding.
47	B	Explain the roles and functions of characters in various plots, including their relationships and conflicts.
48	B	Identify the literary language and devices used in biographies and autobiographies, including how authors present major events in a person's life.
49	A	Evaluate the impact of sensory details, imagery, and figurative language in literary text.
50	B	Determine the meaning of grade-level academic English words derived from Latin, Greek, or other linguistic roots and affixes.

Question	Answer	TEKS Standard
51	C	Identify the literary language and devices used in biographies and autobiographies, including how authors present major events in a person's life.
52	B	Make connections (e.g., thematic links, author analysis) between and across multiple texts of various genres and provide textual evidence.
53	C	Make connections (e.g., thematic links, author analysis) between and across multiple texts of various genres and provide textual evidence.
54	A	Compare and contrast the themes or moral lessons of several works of fiction from various cultures.

Section 4: STAAR Reading Practice Test 2

Practice Test 2, Session 1

Question	Answer	TEKS Standard
1	C	Determine the meaning of grade-level academic English words derived from Latin, Greek, or other linguistic roots and affixes.
2	B	Identify the author's viewpoint or position and explain the basic relationships among ideas in the argument.
3	B	Synthesize and make logical connections between ideas within a text and across two or three texts representing similar or different genres.
4	C	Make inferences about text and use textual evidence to support understanding.
5	A	Draw conclusions from the information presented by an author and evaluate how well the author's purpose was achieved.
6	B	Recognize exaggerated, contradictory, or misleading statements in text.
7	C	Identify the point of view of media presentations.
8	D	Summarize the main ideas and supporting details in a text in ways that maintain meaning and logical order.
9	B	Determine the facts in text and verify them through established methods.
10	B	Use context to determine or clarify the meaning of unfamiliar or multiple meaning words.
11	D	Evaluate the impact of sensory details, imagery, and figurative language in literary text.
12	A	Understand, make inferences and draw conclusions about the structure and elements of drama and provide evidence from text to support their understanding.
13	B	Explain the roles and functions of characters in various plots, including their relationships and conflicts.
14	D	Explain different forms of third-person points of view in stories.
15	B	Understand, make inferences and draw conclusions about the structure and elements of drama and provide evidence from text to support their understanding.
16	A	Describe incidents that advance the story or novel, explaining how each incident gives rise to or foreshadows future events.
17	C	Make inferences about text and use textual evidence to support understanding.
18	D	Describe incidents that advance the story or novel, explaining how each incident gives rise to or foreshadows future events.
19	B	Summarize the main ideas and supporting details in a text in ways that maintain meaning and logical order.
20	A	Synthesize and make logical connections between ideas within a text and across two or three texts representing similar or different genres.

Question	Answer	TEKS Standard
21	B	Summarize and paraphrase texts in ways that maintain meaning and logical order within a text and across texts.
22	D	Analyze how the organizational pattern of a text influences the relationships among the ideas.
23	A	Interpret factual or quantitative information presented in maps, charts, illustrations, graphs, timelines, tables, and diagrams.
24	B	Determine the facts in text and verify them through established methods.
25	D	Interpret factual or quantitative information presented in maps, charts, illustrations, graphs, timelines, tables, and diagrams.
26	C	Use multiple text features and graphics to gain an overview of the contents of text and to locate information.
27	D	Use a dictionary, a glossary, or a thesaurus to determine the meanings, syllabication, pronunciations, alternate word choices, and parts of speech of words.

Practice Test 2, Session 2

Question	Answer	TEKS Standard
28	B	Use context to determine or clarify the meaning of unfamiliar or multiple meaning words.
29	C	Determine the meaning of grade-level academic English words derived from Latin, Greek, or other linguistic roots and affixes.
30	C	Make connections (e.g., thematic links, author analysis) between and across multiple texts of various genres and provide textual evidence.
31	C	Describe incidents that advance the story or novel, explaining how each incident gives rise to or foreshadows future events.
32	D	Summarize and paraphrase texts in ways that maintain meaning and logical order within a text and across texts.
33	A	Explain the roles and functions of characters in various plots, including their relationships and conflicts.
34	D	Make inferences about text and use textual evidence to support understanding.
35	C	Describe incidents that advance the story or novel, explaining how each incident gives rise to or foreshadows future events.
36	A	Explain different forms of third-person points of view in stories.
37	C	Use context to determine or clarify the meaning of unfamiliar or multiple meaning words.
38	D	Evaluate the impact of sensory details, imagery, and figurative language in literary text.
39	B	Explain the roles and functions of characters in various plots, including their relationships and conflicts.
40	C	Summarize and paraphrase texts in ways that maintain meaning and logical order within a text and across texts.
41	B	Summarize and paraphrase texts in ways that maintain meaning and logical order within a text and across texts.
42	A	Make inferences about text and use textual evidence to support understanding.
43	B	Identify the literary language and devices used in biographies and autobiographies, including how authors present major events in a person's life.
44	C	Draw conclusions from the information presented by an author and evaluate how well the author's purpose was achieved.
45	B	Analyze how the organizational pattern of a text influences the relationships among the ideas.
46	B	Use multiple text features and graphics to gain an overview of the contents of text and to locate information.
47	A	Use context to determine or clarify the meaning of unfamiliar or multiple meaning words.
48	C	Summarize the main ideas and supporting details in a text in ways that maintain meaning and logical order.
49	D	Use context to determine or clarify the meaning of unfamiliar or multiple meaning words.

Question	Answer	TEKS Standard
50	C	Identify the author's viewpoint or position and explain the basic relationships among ideas in the argument.
51	B	Determine the facts in text and verify them through established methods.
52	A	Synthesize and make logical connections between ideas within a text and across two or three texts representing similar or different genres.
53	B	Make connections (e.g., thematic links, author analysis) between and across multiple texts of various genres and provide textual evidence.
54	B	Make connections (e.g., thematic links, author analysis) between and across multiple texts of various genres and provide textual evidence.

Section 1: Reading Mini-Tests

Mini-Test 1		Mini-Test 2		Mini-Test 3	
1	Ⓐ Ⓑ Ⓒ Ⓓ	1	Ⓐ Ⓑ Ⓒ Ⓓ	1	Ⓐ Ⓑ Ⓒ Ⓓ
2	Ⓐ Ⓑ Ⓒ Ⓓ	2	Ⓐ Ⓑ Ⓒ Ⓓ	2	Ⓐ Ⓑ Ⓒ Ⓓ
3	Ⓐ Ⓑ Ⓒ Ⓓ	3	Ⓐ Ⓑ Ⓒ Ⓓ	3	Ⓐ Ⓑ Ⓒ Ⓓ
4	Ⓐ Ⓑ Ⓒ Ⓓ	4	Ⓐ Ⓑ Ⓒ Ⓓ	4	Ⓐ Ⓑ Ⓒ Ⓓ
5	Ⓐ Ⓑ Ⓒ Ⓓ	5	Ⓐ Ⓑ Ⓒ Ⓓ	5	Ⓐ Ⓑ Ⓒ Ⓓ
6	Ⓐ Ⓑ Ⓒ Ⓓ	6	Ⓐ Ⓑ Ⓒ Ⓓ	6	Ⓐ Ⓑ Ⓒ Ⓓ
7	Ⓐ Ⓑ Ⓒ Ⓓ	7	Ⓐ Ⓑ Ⓒ Ⓓ	7	Ⓐ Ⓑ Ⓒ Ⓓ
8	Ⓐ Ⓑ Ⓒ Ⓓ	8	Ⓐ Ⓑ Ⓒ Ⓓ	8	Ⓐ Ⓑ Ⓒ Ⓓ
9	Ⓐ Ⓑ Ⓒ Ⓓ	9	Ⓐ Ⓑ Ⓒ Ⓓ	9	Ⓐ Ⓑ Ⓒ Ⓓ
10	Ⓐ Ⓑ Ⓒ Ⓓ	10	Ⓐ Ⓑ Ⓒ Ⓓ	10	Ⓐ Ⓑ Ⓒ Ⓓ

Mini-Test 4		Mini-Test 5		Mini-Test 6	
1	Ⓐ Ⓑ Ⓒ Ⓓ	1	Ⓐ Ⓑ Ⓒ Ⓓ	1	Ⓐ Ⓑ Ⓒ Ⓓ
2	Ⓐ Ⓑ Ⓒ Ⓓ	2	Ⓐ Ⓑ Ⓒ Ⓓ	2	Ⓐ Ⓑ Ⓒ Ⓓ
3	Ⓐ Ⓑ Ⓒ Ⓓ	3	Ⓐ Ⓑ Ⓒ Ⓓ	3	Ⓐ Ⓑ Ⓒ Ⓓ
4	Ⓐ Ⓑ Ⓒ Ⓓ	4	Ⓐ Ⓑ Ⓒ Ⓓ	4	Ⓐ Ⓑ Ⓒ Ⓓ
5	Ⓐ Ⓑ Ⓒ Ⓓ	5	Ⓐ Ⓑ Ⓒ Ⓓ	5	Ⓐ Ⓑ Ⓒ Ⓓ
6	Ⓐ Ⓑ Ⓒ Ⓓ	6	Ⓐ Ⓑ Ⓒ Ⓓ	6	Ⓐ Ⓑ Ⓒ Ⓓ
7	Ⓐ Ⓑ Ⓒ Ⓓ	7	Ⓐ Ⓑ Ⓒ Ⓓ	7	Ⓐ Ⓑ Ⓒ Ⓓ
8	Ⓐ Ⓑ Ⓒ Ⓓ	8	Ⓐ Ⓑ Ⓒ Ⓓ	8	Ⓐ Ⓑ Ⓒ Ⓓ
9	Ⓐ Ⓑ Ⓒ Ⓓ	9	Ⓐ Ⓑ Ⓒ Ⓓ	9	Ⓐ Ⓑ Ⓒ Ⓓ
10	Ⓐ Ⓑ Ⓒ Ⓓ	10	Ⓐ Ⓑ Ⓒ Ⓓ	10	Ⓐ Ⓑ Ⓒ Ⓓ
		11	Ⓐ Ⓑ Ⓒ Ⓓ	11	Ⓐ Ⓑ Ⓒ Ⓓ
		12	Ⓐ Ⓑ Ⓒ Ⓓ	12	Ⓐ Ⓑ Ⓒ Ⓓ

Section 2: Vocabulary Quizzes

Quiz 1		Quiz 2		Quiz 3	
1	Ⓐ Ⓑ Ⓒ Ⓓ	1	Ⓐ Ⓑ Ⓒ Ⓓ	1	Ⓐ Ⓑ Ⓒ Ⓓ
2	Ⓐ Ⓑ Ⓒ Ⓓ	2	Ⓐ Ⓑ Ⓒ Ⓓ	2	Ⓐ Ⓑ Ⓒ Ⓓ
3	Ⓐ Ⓑ Ⓒ Ⓓ	3	Ⓐ Ⓑ Ⓒ Ⓓ	3	Ⓐ Ⓑ Ⓒ Ⓓ
4	Ⓐ Ⓑ Ⓒ Ⓓ	4	Ⓐ Ⓑ Ⓒ Ⓓ	4	Ⓐ Ⓑ Ⓒ Ⓓ
5	Ⓐ Ⓑ Ⓒ Ⓓ	5	Ⓐ Ⓑ Ⓒ Ⓓ	5	Ⓐ Ⓑ Ⓒ Ⓓ
6	Ⓐ Ⓑ Ⓒ Ⓓ	6	Ⓐ Ⓑ Ⓒ Ⓓ	6	Ⓐ Ⓑ Ⓒ Ⓓ
7	Ⓐ Ⓑ Ⓒ Ⓓ			7	Ⓐ Ⓑ Ⓒ Ⓓ
8	Ⓐ Ⓑ Ⓒ Ⓓ			8	Ⓐ Ⓑ Ⓒ Ⓓ
9	Ⓐ Ⓑ Ⓒ Ⓓ				

Quiz 4		Quiz 5		Quiz 6	
1	Ⓐ Ⓑ Ⓒ Ⓓ	1	Ⓐ Ⓑ Ⓒ Ⓓ	1	Ⓐ Ⓑ Ⓒ Ⓓ
2	Ⓐ Ⓑ Ⓒ Ⓓ	2	Ⓐ Ⓑ Ⓒ Ⓓ	2	Ⓐ Ⓑ Ⓒ Ⓓ
3	Ⓐ Ⓑ Ⓒ Ⓓ	3	Ⓐ Ⓑ Ⓒ Ⓓ	3	Ⓐ Ⓑ Ⓒ Ⓓ
4	Ⓐ Ⓑ Ⓒ Ⓓ	4	Ⓐ Ⓑ Ⓒ Ⓓ	4	Ⓐ Ⓑ Ⓒ Ⓓ
5	Ⓐ Ⓑ Ⓒ Ⓓ	5	Ⓐ Ⓑ Ⓒ Ⓓ	5	Ⓐ Ⓑ Ⓒ Ⓓ
6	Ⓐ Ⓑ Ⓒ Ⓓ	6	Ⓐ Ⓑ Ⓒ Ⓓ		
7	Ⓐ Ⓑ Ⓒ Ⓓ	7	Ⓐ Ⓑ Ⓒ Ⓓ		
8	Ⓐ Ⓑ Ⓒ Ⓓ				

Section 3: STAAR Reading Practice Test 1

STAAR Reading Practice Test 1: Session 1

1	Ⓐ Ⓑ Ⓒ Ⓓ	10	Ⓐ Ⓑ Ⓒ Ⓓ	19	Ⓐ Ⓑ Ⓒ Ⓓ
2	Ⓐ Ⓑ Ⓒ Ⓓ	11	Ⓐ Ⓑ Ⓒ Ⓓ	20	Ⓐ Ⓑ Ⓒ Ⓓ
3	Ⓐ Ⓑ Ⓒ Ⓓ	12	Ⓐ Ⓑ Ⓒ Ⓓ	21	Ⓐ Ⓑ Ⓒ Ⓓ
4	Ⓐ Ⓑ Ⓒ Ⓓ	13	Ⓐ Ⓑ Ⓒ Ⓓ	22	Ⓐ Ⓑ Ⓒ Ⓓ
5	Ⓐ Ⓑ Ⓒ Ⓓ	14	Ⓐ Ⓑ Ⓒ Ⓓ	23	Ⓐ Ⓑ Ⓒ Ⓓ
6	Ⓐ Ⓑ Ⓒ Ⓓ	15	Ⓐ Ⓑ Ⓒ Ⓓ	24	Ⓐ Ⓑ Ⓒ Ⓓ
7	Ⓐ Ⓑ Ⓒ Ⓓ	16	Ⓐ Ⓑ Ⓒ Ⓓ	25	Ⓐ Ⓑ Ⓒ Ⓓ
8	Ⓐ Ⓑ Ⓒ Ⓓ	17	Ⓐ Ⓑ Ⓒ Ⓓ	26	Ⓐ Ⓑ Ⓒ Ⓓ
9	Ⓐ Ⓑ Ⓒ Ⓓ	18	Ⓐ Ⓑ Ⓒ Ⓓ	27	Ⓐ Ⓑ Ⓒ Ⓓ

STAAR Reading Practice Test 1: Session 2

28	Ⓐ Ⓑ Ⓒ Ⓓ	37	Ⓐ Ⓑ Ⓒ Ⓓ	46	Ⓐ Ⓑ Ⓒ Ⓓ
29	Ⓐ Ⓑ Ⓒ Ⓓ	38	Ⓐ Ⓑ Ⓒ Ⓓ	47	Ⓐ Ⓑ Ⓒ Ⓓ
30	Ⓐ Ⓑ Ⓒ Ⓓ	39	Ⓐ Ⓑ Ⓒ Ⓓ	48	Ⓐ Ⓑ Ⓒ Ⓓ
31	Ⓐ Ⓑ Ⓒ Ⓓ	40	Ⓐ Ⓑ Ⓒ Ⓓ	49	Ⓐ Ⓑ Ⓒ Ⓓ
32	Ⓐ Ⓑ Ⓒ Ⓓ	41	Ⓐ Ⓑ Ⓒ Ⓓ	50	Ⓐ Ⓑ Ⓒ Ⓓ
33	Ⓐ Ⓑ Ⓒ Ⓓ	42	Ⓐ Ⓑ Ⓒ Ⓓ	51	Ⓐ Ⓑ Ⓒ Ⓓ
34	Ⓐ Ⓑ Ⓒ Ⓓ	43	Ⓐ Ⓑ Ⓒ Ⓓ	52	Ⓐ Ⓑ Ⓒ Ⓓ
35	Ⓐ Ⓑ Ⓒ Ⓓ	44	Ⓐ Ⓑ Ⓒ Ⓓ	53	Ⓐ Ⓑ Ⓒ Ⓓ
36	Ⓐ Ⓑ Ⓒ Ⓓ	45	Ⓐ Ⓑ Ⓒ Ⓓ	54	Ⓐ Ⓑ Ⓒ Ⓓ

Section 4: STAAR Reading Practice Test 2

STAAR Reading Practice Test 2: Session 1

1	Ⓐ Ⓑ Ⓒ Ⓓ	10	Ⓐ Ⓑ Ⓒ Ⓓ	19	Ⓐ Ⓑ Ⓒ Ⓓ
2	Ⓐ Ⓑ Ⓒ Ⓓ	11	Ⓐ Ⓑ Ⓒ Ⓓ	20	Ⓐ Ⓑ Ⓒ Ⓓ
3	Ⓐ Ⓑ Ⓒ Ⓓ	12	Ⓐ Ⓑ Ⓒ Ⓓ	21	Ⓐ Ⓑ Ⓒ Ⓓ
4	Ⓐ Ⓑ Ⓒ Ⓓ	13	Ⓐ Ⓑ Ⓒ Ⓓ	22	Ⓐ Ⓑ Ⓒ Ⓓ
5	Ⓐ Ⓑ Ⓒ Ⓓ	14	Ⓐ Ⓑ Ⓒ Ⓓ	23	Ⓐ Ⓑ Ⓒ Ⓓ
6	Ⓐ Ⓑ Ⓒ Ⓓ	15	Ⓐ Ⓑ Ⓒ Ⓓ	24	Ⓐ Ⓑ Ⓒ Ⓓ
7	Ⓐ Ⓑ Ⓒ Ⓓ	16	Ⓐ Ⓑ Ⓒ Ⓓ	25	Ⓐ Ⓑ Ⓒ Ⓓ
8	Ⓐ Ⓑ Ⓒ Ⓓ	17	Ⓐ Ⓑ Ⓒ Ⓓ	26	Ⓐ Ⓑ Ⓒ Ⓓ
9	Ⓐ Ⓑ Ⓒ Ⓓ	18	Ⓐ Ⓑ Ⓒ Ⓓ	27	Ⓐ Ⓑ Ⓒ Ⓓ

STAAR Reading Practice Test 2: Session 2

28	Ⓐ Ⓑ Ⓒ Ⓓ	37	Ⓐ Ⓑ Ⓒ Ⓓ	46	Ⓐ Ⓑ Ⓒ Ⓓ
29	Ⓐ Ⓑ Ⓒ Ⓓ	38	Ⓐ Ⓑ Ⓒ Ⓓ	47	Ⓐ Ⓑ Ⓒ Ⓓ
30	Ⓐ Ⓑ Ⓒ Ⓓ	39	Ⓐ Ⓑ Ⓒ Ⓓ	48	Ⓐ Ⓑ Ⓒ Ⓓ
31	Ⓐ Ⓑ Ⓒ Ⓓ	40	Ⓐ Ⓑ Ⓒ Ⓓ	49	Ⓐ Ⓑ Ⓒ Ⓓ
32	Ⓐ Ⓑ Ⓒ Ⓓ	41	Ⓐ Ⓑ Ⓒ Ⓓ	50	Ⓐ Ⓑ Ⓒ Ⓓ
33	Ⓐ Ⓑ Ⓒ Ⓓ	42	Ⓐ Ⓑ Ⓒ Ⓓ	51	Ⓐ Ⓑ Ⓒ Ⓓ
34	Ⓐ Ⓑ Ⓒ Ⓓ	43	Ⓐ Ⓑ Ⓒ Ⓓ	52	Ⓐ Ⓑ Ⓒ Ⓓ
35	Ⓐ Ⓑ Ⓒ Ⓓ	44	Ⓐ Ⓑ Ⓒ Ⓓ	53	Ⓐ Ⓑ Ⓒ Ⓓ
36	Ⓐ Ⓑ Ⓒ Ⓓ	45	Ⓐ Ⓑ Ⓒ Ⓓ	54	Ⓐ Ⓑ Ⓒ Ⓓ

Made in the USA
Coppell, TX
30 October 2019